Through Julian's Windows

Through
Julian's Windows

Contemplating Whatever-God with
Julian of Norwich

Elizabeth Ruth Obbard

GRACEWING

Through Julian's Windows

Growing into Wholeness with
Julian of Norwich

Elizabeth Ruth Obbard

CANTERBURY
PRESS
Norwich

© Elizabeth Ruth Obbard 2008

First published in 2008 by the Canterbury Press Norwich
(a publishing imprint of Hymns Ancient & Modern Limited,
a registered charity)
13–17 Long Lane, London EC1A 9PN

www.scm-canterburypress.co.uk

British Library Cataloguing in Publication data

A catalogue record for this book is available
from the British Library

ISBN 978-1-85311-903-3

Typeset by Regent Typesetting, London
Printed in the UK by CPI Bookmarque, Croydon, CR0 4TD

In memory of Br John Berridge O.Carm,

a man of compassion
greatly loving and greatly loved

*'[He] walked with God; then he was no more,
because God took him'*

Genesis 5.24

and for Bill

Contents

Contents

Prologue

Julian – A Woman of Yesterday for Today

*I*n the late fourteenth century a woman sat at a small table writing.* Her single room (or cell) was built on to the side of the Church of St Julian in the commercial district of Norwich. The room possessed three windows: one looked on to the sanctuary of the church; one communicated with a maid who ran errands and attended to simple household tasks; the other window, covered by a black curtain with a white cross embroidered on it, was where the woman received those who came to ask for counsel. Inside a small porch, to keep out of the way of inclement weather, people could seat themselves in a modicum of privacy and pour out their troubled hearts to someone who was their local sister and friend. She received all without distinction – the distraught widow who had lost husband and child to the plague; the boatman plying his wares from abroad and seeking a motherly heart to remind him of home; the prostitute who walked

---

* The quotations from the *Revelations of Divine Love* (RDL) by Julian of Norwich are taken from the unpublished translation of the Paris Manuscript by Josef Pischler MHM, edited by E. R. Obbard.

brazenly or shamefacedly in the nearby red-light district, and who wanted a kind word that did not pass judgement but sought to understand that sometimes this was the only way for a woman to support her children; the priest in the toils of a love affair that had to be kept secret; the ordinary Christian seeking to know God's will when life was hard and poverty ever present.

At night, with the approach of darkness, the anchoress, for such the woman was, would stealthily unbolt the servant's door and take a little time to walk in the church-yard, breathing the dark air and watching the stars blinking a greeting to her in the wide Norfolk sky. If she was fortunate she might even catch sight of an orange and purple sunset, or a puffy pink sunrise suffusing the horizon of roofs and spires in the early morning before others were up.

When her servant brought her herrings from the market she would be reminded of her vision of the crucifix; and if the weather was bad she would watch the rain coursing down the roof of her cell and dropping on to the ground from the eaves, just as blood had seemed to stream from the figure on the cross that had once spoken to her when she lay dying, as she thought, at the age of 30.

During the whole time that our Lord showed me this spiritual vision . . . I saw with my bodily eyes the head of Christ continuously bleeding. The great drops of blood fell down under the crown of thorns like pellets, which looked as if they had come from the veins. When they came out they were brownish-red in colour (for the blood was very thick) and as they spread they were bright red. Then when they reached the eyebrows they vanished. Yet the bleeding continued until I had seen and understood many things. Nevertheless, the beautiful and lifelike head continued in the same beauty without diminishing.

The abundance was like the drops of water that fall off the eaves of a roof after a heavy shower of rain, falling so thickly that it is beyond human skill to count them. And as they spread out on the forehead they were as round as herrings' scales.

These three images came to my mind at that time:

Pellets because of the roundness of the drops of blood when they first appeared.

Herrings' scales because of the roundness spreading on the forehead.

Raindrops falling from the eaves of a house, because they were too many to count.

This vision was real and lifelike, horrifying and fearful, sweet and lovely. And what gave me most encouragement in the whole vision was the knowledge that our good Lord, who is so holy and fearful, is also so homely and courteous. And it is this that most filled my soul with delight and assurance.

RDL 7.2–5

But death had not prevailed at this point in the woman's life. She lived to tell of what she had seen and all that it had come to mean to her over the years. As she wrote even now she was exploring the meaning ever more deeply, so that she could share with others what she had learned in those few packed hours when she thought life was over and eternity dawning.

Then I said to those around me: 'Today is my Day of Judgement.' I said this because I thought I was about to die. And I believe that on the day we die we are judged as we will be for ever. I said this too because I wished that [those around me] would love our Lord better, and to remind them that this life is short (as they might see in my case). For all the time I was certain that I was about to die.

This filled me with wonder, but it also half disturbed me, because I thought that this vision was given for those who were meant to live.

Everything I am saying about myself I mean to say for all my fellow Christians, for I was taught in the spiritual vision that this is what our Lord intends. Therefore I beg you all for God's sake, and advise you for your own benefit, that you stop thinking about the poor wretch to whom the vision was shown, and that you wholeheartedly, powerfully and wisely contemplate God, who in his courteous love and in his endless goodness wanted to show these things to all, so that all might be comforted. It is God's will that you accept it with the greatest joy and delight as if Jesus himself had shown it to you.

RDL 8.4–5

The sight was Julian's alone. The insight was for all. She had been entrusted with a mission and was determined to share it in whatever way she could. Hence the writing, the thinking, the praying, the solitary life she led beside the church.

The lady at St Julian's was not the only person in Norwich living a solitary life. At every city gate an enclosed man or woman collected tolls; at almost every church a small cell abbutted the sanctuary for others living like herself. It was a simple lifestyle, easily supported by local people, with none of the management of estates and benefices that made conventual or monastic life a heavy administrative burden for those responsible for religious communities.

But this grey-clad woman was different from those who, like herself, lived lives of retirement within the city walls. Even as she wrote she was anonymous. She was simply 'the lady at St Julian's', soon to be shortened to 'the Lady Julian'. People would forget her family circumstances, her original place of residence, her youth and early maturity, all that made her an individual with a specific past. She was fast becoming a spiritual guide and mother, an anchor holding firm in the storms of a tumultuous history from which she was removed by her calling.

This woman might smell the fires not far from her cell where the followers of Wyclif were burned for heresy, but her work was to persevere in prayer, not engage in controversy. She was called to transformation of self in Christ, not reformation of others.

Our Lord is very happy and glad with our prayer. He expects it and wants to have it, because with his grace it makes us as like himself in condition as we are in nature . . . Because of the reward and endless thanks God wants to give, he desires to have us constantly praying before him. God accepts the good intentions and efforts of his servants, regardless of our feelings. Therefore it pleases him to see us at work both in prayer and good living, with his help and grace, directing all our faculties to him intelligently and with discretion, until we possess in complete joy the one we seek – Jesus himself.

RDL 41.4–5

The Lady Julian was the one who would take others to God in silent prayer, and share with those who came to her not only her insights but also the alms she had received for sustenance. Her maids, Sarah and Alice, were familiar figures in the streets of the town, purchasing grain and bread, collecting gifts of vegetables, fruit and fish from the market stalls, distributing needlework in the form of garments made for the poor. What was left from the daily meal was available for any who might come to Julian's window and hold out a hopeful hand.

This woman is known to history as Julian of Norwich. Her cell has been rebuilt on its original foundations and has become a place of peace and prayer. Even today Julian welcomes those who come as pilgrims to her simple dwelling, and shares with them something of the secret of her understanding of God and the human heart, summed up in the last chapter of her book, written after many years of pondering and praying.

From the time I first had these revelations I often longed to know what our Lord meant. More than fifteen years later I was given in response a spiritual understanding.

I was told: 'Do you want to know what our Lord meant in all this? Know it well – Love was his meaning.

Who showed it to you? Love.

What did he show you? Love.

Why did he show it to you? For love.

Remain firm in this love and you will taste it ever more deeply.

But you will never know anything else from it for ever and ever.'

So I was taught that love was what our Lord meant. And I saw with absolute certainty in this revelation and

in all the rest, that before God made us he loved us, and
that this love never slackened nor ever shall. In his love
he has done all his works; in his love he has made all
things for our benefit; and in this love our life is everlasting. In our creation we had a beginning, but the love
in which he created us was in him for ever and without
beginning. In this love we have our beginning.

And all this we shall see in God without end.

RDL 86.3–4

Julian's loving words of wisdom are still heard through
her writings. She is a beacon of hope and a model for those
called to the ministry of prayer and counsel, especially
those who follow in some way a lifestyle similar to her
own.

I do not speak here of anchoresses per se. I refer to the
modern-day solitaries and hermits, often like Julian in an
urban setting, away from the support of a monastic or
religious community, yet seeking God in singleness of
heart and in the encounters that happen in the course of
daily life. Such people, like most who try to live a spiritual
life, have three windows on to the world: the window
of prayer; the window of practicalities; and the window of
presence to others; and all three are interconnected.

Julian can teach us how to balance the conflicting
demands on our time, but she can also teach us how to
nourish our own inner solitude while befriending others
and holding them close in prayer and compassion. She
teaches us how to turn our 'desert of loneliness' into a
hospitable 'garden of solitude', as Henri Nouwen defines
the inner journey. We can be, as Julian was, 'wounded
healers' in a fragmented world, through the three things
that she herself prayed for as wounds and discovered to

be medicines for healing: contrition, compassion, and longing for God. With these three 'wounds that heal' we are offered windows into ourselves and into the mystery of others. Thus we are nourished and strengthened in our own spiritual life and can be effective spiritual companions for those who come to us, looking for a word of challenge, of understanding, of acceptance, of hope.

The life of prayer and human compassion is never a one-way journey only. Our lives become entwined with the lives of those we meet, and together we journey deeper into the mystery of God.

Space to Reflect

'I will not leave you orphaned; I am coming to you. In a little while the world will no longer see me, but you will see me; because I live, you also will live . . . They who have my commandments and keep them are those who love me; and those who love me will be loved by my Father, and I will love them and reveal myself to them.'

John 14.18–19, 21

Sight and Insight

Julian is not someone who has a whole lifetime of successive visionary experiences. Rather, she is a woman who draws upon all she 'sees' with her bodily sight as she lies dying, and from this one experience gives us her 'insights' into the meaning behind it all, especially her insights into the nature of God and the reality of love undergirding all that is.

This kind of experience is not a phenomenon accessible

only to great saints and mystics. It is available to each one of us in our own way and according to our own capacity.

Take a few moments now to think of some experience you have had that opened up new vistas within you; that moved you from sight to insight. Perhaps it was an experience of human love, of the mingled joy and pain of childbirth, of a beautiful scene in nature, or the sudden solution to a problem.

Make a note of what you saw or experienced and what you learned from it. Was it an insight into the nature of reality? Into the love of God? Into a timeless sense of the beauty and tears at the heart of things?

What more is there still to learn from this experience?

Keeping the Vision Alive

Julian knows well enough that we need to keep going back to draw nourishment from our moments of insight, otherwise they get swept away and forgotten as life takes its course. She writes:

> When the revelation, which is given only for a short time, is past and hidden, then grace keeps it alive by the grace of the Holy Spirit, to the end of our lives. So the revelation is nothing else but faith, neither more nor less, as can be seen from the teaching of our Lord in this matter when the revelation is complete.

RDL 7.9

Julian's visions are only understood in the last chapter of her book when she sums everything up as love. Before that she needs to keep going over the same ground again and again.

To have faith in ourselves and our insights is part of having faith in a God who speaks to us and who communicates with us in a variety of ways: through dreams; through our unconscious; through other people; through prayer.

Blessed Angela of Foligno

One of the early Franciscan women, who died some years before Julian's birth, was Angela of Foligno (1244–1309). Angela had been married, but at one point lost her mother, husband and sons in some tragedy. Hers was a long, drawn-out spiritual path as she tried to live for God. She left her comfortable home and became a Franciscan Tertiary, living a solitary life of prayer and service with a companion. But as the years passed she became 'mother and teacher' to a group of followers who recognized her giftedness in the things of the spirit. Angela was sustained by a number of 'seeings' and 'in-seeings' centred upon the Passion and the Franciscan ideal of Christ poor, naked and suffering. Her spirituality is more emotional, more out of the ordinary, than Julian's. But she is an example of how God leads each one along the way that best accords with his or her own nature and temperament. At one point, Angela 'sees' the whole creation lit up from within, causing her to exclaim in wonder, 'This world is pregnant with God!'

Take time to look out of the window or walk in the garden and see there how God is manifest in and through creation, a creation 'pregnant with God' waiting to give birth to 'something more' in your seeing and 'in-seeing'.

Scriptural Meditation

[Jacob] dreamed that there was a ladder set up on the earth, the top of it reaching to heaven; and the angels of God were ascending and descending on it . . . Then Jacob woke from his sleep and said, 'Surely the Lord is in this place – and I did not know it! This is none other than the house of God, and this is the gate of heaven.'

Genesis 28.12, 16–17

Prayer

Pilgrim God,
bring my soul into harmony with you.
Let there be no false harmony in me,
such as saying I want you
but not really meaning it.
Give me the desire that brings my whole body
into harmony with my soul.
Bring my soul into harmony with my heart,
that I may become truly at one with you
and with the whole of creation.
Thus you will be my companion on the way
and the friend who meets me at the end of my journey.

Prayer based on the words of Angela of Foligno

A Window on to History: The Vocation to Solitude

Biblical Foundations

*T*he hermit life in the Church has a long history, reaching back into the Hebrew Scriptures, where we find the prophets readying themselves for their task by times of withdrawal, either physical or spiritual, usually both. To hear the word of God and convey it to others means a willingness to listen to the Other, and a purity of heart that enables the Word to be communicated with a force drawn from outside the self.

The desert sojourn of Israel was a time when God seemed to be particularly close. It was a time when the people entered into the Covenant, accepting to be God's people and to live in God's way. The journey through the wilderness was always looked back on as the 'honeymoon' period of Israelite history, when all other landmarks had disappeared and the Israelites learned to rely on God alone rather than their own insights and efforts.

> I remember the devotion of your youth, your love as a bride,

how you followed me in the wilderness, in a land not
sown.

Jeremiah 2.2

Therefore, I will now persuade her,
and bring her into the wilderness,
and speak tenderly to her.
From there I will give her her vineyards,
and make the Valley of Achor a door of hope.
There she shall respond as in the days of her youth, as at
the time when she came out of the land of Egypt.

Hosea 2.14–15

Solitude in the Hebrew mind is a component of listening
to and relying on the God who speaks to us. From the
early days of Christianity, the prophet Elijah was considered the archetype of the solitary vocation. He 'turns
eastwards' to hide by the Wadi Cherith, being fed by
ravens and drinking from the brook, dependent on the
providence of God in his necessity (1 Kings 17.3–7). It is
Elijah who, in fleeing from Jezebel after confronting the
false prophets of Baal, goes into the desert to Mount
Horeb, and there encounters God in the 'sound of sheer
silence' (1 Kings 19.11–12). But Elijah is not only a man
of prayer. He is a man of action, called to minister to
others with compassion, to proclaim the word of God's
justice, to anoint a successor who will carry on his mission.

So we have in this model of the solitary life an element
of presence to self, to others and to God. Presence to self
through learning to live alone in the desert and there discover who one is and what one is called to do, to be and to
become. Presence to others, in that Elijah is one who
discerns when he must act with and for those in need.

Presence to God in an underlying current of prayer – a listening to God's word in whatever way it comes to him through the circumstances of his life as they unfold.

John the Baptist, the New Testament Elijah, is a desert dweller who has the courage to confront, to call to repentance, and ultimately give his life as a lone voice for the truth. He prepares the way of the Lord so that others may also encounter God and respond to God's demands.

In both these models of the hermit life there is an element of the desert, of withdrawal from ordinary human intercourse. But there is also an element of involvement in the history of the Israelite nation that is an outcome of knowing oneself and knowing God.

These elements can be discerned in the eremitical vocation throughout history, but they are not meant to be replicated by a mechanical imitation. As we shall see, the solitary life has taken different forms throughout the history of the Church, and with a differing balance of prayer, solitude and presence to others in the lives of hermits themselves.

The Desert Fathers and Mothers

The desert fathers and mothers developed from a movement that wanted to keep a radical form of commitment to Christ before the eyes of a Church that was rapidly becoming a community fuelled by values that were the antithesis of those promoted by her founder. Once the era of the martyrs was over and Christianity became the religion of the Empire it was only to be expected that the values of the Empire should prevail. The movement to the desert was a movement that wanted to make a strong distinction between the values of the world at large and the values of Christ as depicted in the gospel. The hermit was to bear witness, like John the Baptist, to the essential otherness of the Kingdom of God.

Yet the desert fathers and mothers strike us as balanced and compassionate guides, whatever may have been their personal, and in some cases extreme, asceticism. Living in the desert highlights one's inner poverty. One discovers one's lack of resources when the things one has come to rely upon are stripped away. Hence the practical and blunt advice that desert dwellers are able to impart. For example:

> A brother asked an old man: 'What is humility?' And the old man said: 'To do good to those who hurt you.' The brother said: 'If you cannot go that far what should you do?' The old man replied: 'Get away from them and keep your mouth shut.'

> Saint Syncletia said: 'Just as a treasure exposed is quickly spent, so also any virtue that becomes famous or well publicized vanishes. Just as wax is quickly melted by fire, so the soul is emptied by praise, and loses firmness of virtue.'

> Abba Poemen said to Abba Joseph: 'Tell me how I can become a monk.' And he replied: 'If you want to find rest here and hereafter, say on every occasion, Who am I? And do not judge anybody.'[1]

Monasticism

Many of the early desert fathers and mothers became founders of communities who gathered round them as their influence spread. Thus we have the beginning of monastic life. Many of the early monastic Rules allowed members to choose either to live in a community with others or to follow a solitary lifestyle within a community setting. Such monasteries have continued in the Orthodox Churches. In the West, however, community life under the Rule of St Benedict gradually prevailed, with its emphasis on communal living under an abbot or abbess who was also the spiritual leader of the group. Within the community there was an ordered timetable focused on the chanting of the Divine Office (the 'Work of God'), manual labour and holy reading (*lectio divina*). Various brothers or sisters were in charge of the practical side of life, such as care of the sick, welcoming travellers and pilgrims, preparing meals, and so on. Most monasteries also educated young people in their schools and were the vehicles of preserving and fostering learning.

The Hermit Life in the Early Middle Ages

However, the eremitical life continued in a number of forms quite distinct from monasticism. Hermits or recluses might be former monks or nuns, but often they were lay men and women. In fact, the life showed an astonishing degree of flexibility in respecting the freedom of individuals.

The life of a hermit or recluse was considered to be a form of solidarity with all humanity in that the first principle of the life was acceptance of the human condition, that of being a sinner in need of redemption through union with Christ. It was usually a humane and balanced way of life, which was intended to keep alive the desire for God and service of one's neighbour in a way that could be adjusted to individual need. Harsh penance, even when practised in some cases, was never considered an essential element of the vocation. Rather, the individual response to grace was paramount.

St Francis and the Mendicants

In the thirteenth century, St Francis of Assisi gave new impetus to the hermit life in his interpretation of the '*vita apostolica*' or apostolic way of life followed by Jesus and his apostles. Francis was part of the Europe influenced by the Crusades and the new urban culture. He saw that the monasteries were not meeting the needs of the people and he tried to rectify this through a life where the witness of poverty, prayer and closeness to others was brought out of the cloister and made available to the wider world.

To sustain this life of apostolic labour, travelling and preaching, Francis would alternate periods of intense activity with periods of solitude in the hills around Assisi, where he would concentrate on the life of prayer and union with God. He even wrote his own Rule for Hermits, supposing that the eremitical lifestyle would be relevant for his friars at least from time to time.

It was an era that saw a revival of the solitary life, either in its reclusive form or in the form of pilgrimage, especially among lay men and women, often inspired by the example of Francis, or of other mendicant Orders that sprang up in the wake of his movement. The Carmelite, Servite and Augustinian Recollect friars all looked to eremitical groups as their original inspiration. Also, while by this time the enclosure of nuns was almost universal, both women and men could appropriate the spirituality of the new Orders and live it out in their own personal way, often semi-officially, through the Tertiary associations which allowed greater freedom in interpreting the original vision of the founder. Angela of Foligno, Margaret of Cortona, Jane of Signa, are all examples of women choosing to live the Franciscan charism in ways that were specific to themselves, with varying amounts of solitude, prayer and apostolic outreach.

Solitaries were supposed to live simply, poorly and prayerfully in direct imitation of Christ. It was especially appealing for women, as the number of convents was small and dowries were expected from those who entered, something only the upper classes could afford to provide.

The Life of Reclusion in the Time of Julian

Julian lived in the England of the fourteenth century when the hermit life was at its zenith. All the English mystical writers of the period were in some way connected to the eremitical life. Julian herself was an anchoress, Richard Rolle was a wandering hermit, Walter Hilton wrote *The Ladder of Perfection* for a recluse, and the unknown author of *The Cloud of Unknowing* wrote for a young man setting out on the hermit path. In Norwich alone there were about thirty hermits or recluses contemporary with Julian.

At this point the Church in England was at a low ebb

spiritually. The Black Death had decimated the inmates of religious houses, and to boost numbers it seems that unsuitable candidates were being accepted. For women, the solitary life offered contemplation with an element of freedom and privacy unavailable in convent living. There were far fewer communities of women than men, and a recluse could be supported financially by the local people whose 'sister' she was, ever ready to counsel and pray for those who came to her window. A dowry was not necessary in this instance. She could earn her own living by needlework or teaching small children, as well as accepting gifts in kind.

England, particularly, was open to the hermit and anchoritic vocation. It seems to have suited the English temperament, and such people were honoured and protected by law, taking their place in religious processions directly after the bishop.

The *Ancrene Riwle* (or Rule for Anchoresses), written for three blood sisters in the Salisbury area, shows great latitude in relation to food, drink, clothing, intercourse with others, mutual charity and practical living arrangements. While men might be roving hermits like Richard Rolle – preaching, receiving travellers, keeping roads and bridges in good repair – women were expected for safety's sake to remain in towns, so that their 'desert' was not the external wilderness but the inner path of prayer, 'walled about with God' in a specific location.

The hermit life was always a chosen vocation, subject to discernment by the bishop. One did not just 'become a hermit' by virtue of living alone. Its marks were the imitation of Christ, prayer in solitude, intercession for all, simple work, counsel when sought. In some cases a recluse or hermit would take the prophetic role, seeing from within their solitude where society needed reform or challenge.

In Julian we see a woman who challenges, who speaks, who counsels, who perseveres in prayer, and who weaves into her own life the lives of those among whom she lives and ministers – her 'even Christians'.

The Hermit Life after the Reformation

With the demise of monastic life in England under Henry VIII and the legislation that emanated from the Council of Trent at the Counter Reformation, the hermit life lost its official status in the Church. The Catholic hierarchy questioned whether or not people should be allowed this degree of freedom. If they were drawn to a vocation of prayer and solitude they were persuaded as far as possible to embrace life in a religious Order that fostered eremiticism in a community setting, such as the Carthusians for men or the Carmelite nuns for women. This effectually removed the hermit or recluse from the public eye and cut down any sense of being involved with the local people in a counselling or intercessory role. The loyalty of a monk or nun was primarily to their own community and superior, not to the area in which the monastery was situated.

However, the tradition of *poustiniki* – holy persons living in solitude yet being available to others – continued in the Russian Church, and has been popularized in the West by the writings of Catherine de Huek Docherty. She has done much to introduce some of the Russian traditions to English-speaking countries, and through her Madonna House movement has encouraged many to experience solitude as a path to spiritual growth, with periods of solitude being interspersed with an active apostolic ministry.

The Hermit Life Today

One of the results of the newly revised Canon Law of the Catholic Church is that the vocation of hermit is now officially recognized once more as a specific calling to be lived under the direction of the Diocesan bishop (Canon 603). Other Christian churches are also recognizing and promoting this way of life in both older and more contemporary forms.

Eugene Stockton, an Australian secular priest who came to England to make a study of contemporary hermits, writes that:

> Solitaries themselves I found, as in former times, exhibited a wide variety of states and lifestyles. They were religious belonging to convents and monasteries, parish clergy in active ministry, married couples, business people, retirees, singles in high-rise flats, women babysitting houses, animators of houses of prayer, a priest straddling a place of strict solitude and a place of hospitality, one like a guru or starets seeking and imparting wisdom in an Indian-style ashram, persons on the pilgrimage round of holy places or settled assisting at a holy place, dwellers of lonely locations . . . Many clearly exemplified one of the two stages noted by Marsha Sinetar. She found that such persons display remarkably balanced personalities, and were characterised first by a radical withdrawal from society followed by a 'return to the marketplace', embracing a stewardship of service to others.[2]

The solitary is not a quasi monk or nun out of place in the world, but one who seeks solitude in the midst of, and in communion with, the world. Some live in rhythmic solitude, alternating periods of solitude with periods of greater involvement in an active ministry according to the pattern of a St Francis; others seek a more complete withdrawal. What is important for the person so called is not to strive to conform to a certain definition of hermit, but to seek to answer the call to be alone with God in the given conditions of his or her life.

Relevance for All

Each one of us is in some way solitary as we seek to become self-actualized persons. In each one who is growing towards wholeness there is a need to accept one's aloneness and make it fruitful.

The wounds Julian prayed for – the wounds of contrition, compassion and longing for God – are integral to the way we all must travel as we walk life's pilgrim path as seekers and sojourners. As was quoted in a paper following a symposium on the hermit life after a gathering of modern-day hermits in 1975:

The hermit is simply a pioneer . . . in the way of the desert which the whole of humanity must follow of necessity one day, each one according to the measure of his/her desire. This eremitical vocation, at least embryonically, is to be found in every Christian vocation, but in some it must be allowed to come to its full flowering in the wind of the Spirit. It is not enough to affirm that the thing is good in itself, it is necessary that the Church and society do something, so that this life may be realizable, so that each may at least touch it, be it only with the tip of the little finger.[3]

To live with and for God, to counsel others, to be a sister or brother to those we meet, is the vocation of us all in one degree or another. In this Julian can be our teacher and guide, for she does not threaten or cajole, but inspires and enlightens. She is a friend worth knowing and heeding.

Space to Reflect

But whenever you pray, go into your room and shut the door and pray to your Father who is in secret; and your Father who sees in secret will reward you.

Matthew 6.6

In the morning, while it was still very dark, [Jesus] got up and went out to a deserted place, and there he prayed.

Mark 1.35

Harvesting Hermit Moments

Take some time to consider your own life and how you might harvest some 'hermit moments' in it – a space for God even in the midst of busyness. Eugene Stockton gives some examples of people finding such space when he writes:

There is no reason why a housewife, once she has dropped the children off at school, might not find the next six hours a time to be alone with God, even in the midst of her chores. Likewise the traveller, whether on a prolonged journey or routine commuting, might echo the breviary hymn: 'Alone with none but thee my God I journey on my way.'[4]

To this might be added smaller snatches of time such as while doing the washing up, waiting in the supermarket queue, sitting in a favourite armchair, popping into Church when passing by, or standing quietly in the garden to savour the silence, listening to the sounds of nature while allowing the pressures of life to recede into the background.

Look into your own 'interior room' where you can turn to God whenever you wish and decide on when you will harvest some 'hermit moments' of silent presence and listening during your day.

Our Inner Self

When Julian sees the soul it is interesting that she sees it as a city, most likely modelled on her own city of Norwich, not as a barren desert or even a fruitful garden. In other words, she sees the soul as set within an environment close to her everyday life.

Our good Lord opened my spiritual eyes and showed me my soul in the middle of my heart. I saw the soul as large as if it were an endless citadel and a blessed kingdom. From the conditions that I saw in it I could tell that it is a glorious city. In the midst of that city sits our Lord Jesus, true God and true man . . . The place that Jesus takes in our soul he will never leave again, as I see

[13]

it; for he is our homeliest home and our eternal dwelling.

RDL 68.1, 2

Picture your own soul in whatever setting is helpful to you. Is it a garden, tended or untended? An empty building? A peaceful lake? A city surrounded by a wall? A comfortable living-room?

Write a few words or draw a picture to develop the imagery you have chosen.

Blessed Elizabeth of the Trinity

Blessed Elizabeth of the Trinity (1880–1906), daughter of an army officer and herself a gifted musician, was especially devoted to the thought of God dwelling within her. She developed a spirituality that focused upon this reality even while, as a teenager, she was much in demand for social gatherings and musical performances. Her love of the interior life was something she was very keen to share with her correspondents, even after she became a nun. She writes to a friend who was a wife and mother with many responsibilities:

We possess our heaven within us, since He who satisfies the hunger of the glorified in the light of vision gives Himself to us in faith and mystery, it is the same One! It seems to me that I have found heaven on earth, since Heaven is God, and God is in my soul. The day I understood that, everything became clear to me. I would like to whisper this secret to those I love so they too might always cling to God through everything.[5]

Scriptural Meditation

Those of steadfast mind you keep in peace – in peace because they trust in you. Trust in the Lord for ever, for in the Lord God you have an everlasting rock . . .

My soul yearns for you in the night, my spirit within me earnestly seeks you.

Isaiah 26.3–4, 9

Prayer

Give peace to my soul;
make it your heaven,
your beloved dwelling and your resting place.
May I never leave you there alone, but be wholly
   present,
my faith wholly alert, wholly adoring,
and wholly surrendered to your creative action.

Elizabeth of the Trinity

Notes

1 These examples are all from Nomura, Y., *Desert Wisdom: Sayings from the Desert Fathers*, introduced by Henri Nouwen, Orbis Books, 1982.
2 Stockton, E., 'Lay Hermits', *Compass Theology Review*, vol. 34, no. 2, 2000, pp. 46–50.
3 Allchin, A. M. (ed.), *Solitude and Communion: Papers on the Hermit Life*, SLG Press, 1977, p. 76.
4 Stockton, 'Lay Hermits'.
5 Elizabeth of the Trinity, *Complete Works Volume Two*, trans. Anne Englund Nash, ICS Publications, 1995, p. 51.

2

Wounds as Windows into God and the Self: Julian and her Requests

Julian in Her Time

*W*ho exactly was Julian? There is so much we would like to know about this fascinating woman who has left us a book in two versions, one short and another two-thirds longer. The longer version was written to include the fruit of years of meditation on the insights granted her as she lay close to death on 8 May (or possibly 13 May) 1373.

What we can piece together about Julian is limited to what we can glean from her writings and the environment in which she lived. Julian was born in the year 1342 or thereabouts, a time of great suffering for the English people. Edward III was on the throne, and the Hundred Years War with France was in progress, taking its toll of men and money. The peasants were finding it increasingly difficult to make a living, and their frustration culminated in the Peasants' Revolt of 1381, when the leaders, having been promised a fair hearing, were ruthlessly put down by Henry Despenser, Bishop of Norwich.

When Julian was 7, and again when she was 19 and 27, Norwich was visited by the dreaded Black Death or bubonic plague. People died in droves, the first swellings of the disease in groin or armpit spreading quickly through the body, leading to death the same day. So many died that heaps of bodies would be collected by carts going around the city at night, the carters calling for people to bring out their dead to be buried in great common pits. It is calculated that over a third of the population of England died in outbreaks of bubonic plague, one of them being Julian's contemporary, the wandering hermit and writer, Richard Rolle.

The Church was in a bad state, with the pope moving from Rome to Avignon in the Great Schism and various parts of Christendom supporting various claimants to the papal throne. The Black Death had depleted the monasteries and unsuitable candidates were being accepted, thus lowering the level of regular observance.

In England, John Wyclif translated the Bible into English, for which he was condemned as a heretic. After his death, Lollardy (his followers being nicknamed Lollards) became a capital offence. From her anchorhold in the city Julian would have been able to smell the burning bodies and hear the agonized cries of those tied to the stake in the Lollard pits just outside the city.

So Julian's era was one of poverty, suffering, civil unrest, war and revolt. But it was also a time when Norwich as a city was growing in importance. We think of East Anglia today as a rather out-of-the-way part of England. In Julian's time this was not so at all. The land was farmed intensively and was the centre of the wool trade, famous for its worsted cloth. Money from wool built magnificent churches in every small Norfolk village, besides a number of shrines and places of international pilgrimage – Walsingham, Bromholm, Norwich.

Norwich was deemed to be the second city of the realm after London. Its focal point was the Cathedral of the Holy Trinity, but there were many religious houses within its walls, as well as parish churches, guild chapels and anchorholds. With the Hundred Years War in progress, ports on the south coast were considered dangerous because of their proximity to France, whereas Norfolk ports such as Lyn and Blakeney were extremely busy. Norwich was considered especially safe for export and import, being accessible by river but well inland, away from possible coastal attacks. There was a cosmopolitan atmosphere, with many languages spoken besides English – Latin, French, Flemish, Dutch.

In the Middle Ages religious and secular life were closely intertwined. With the ever-present threat of death and sickness, the Church was at hand with its image of the Crucified Christ to comfort and strengthen the sufferer. A painting of the crucifixion dating from Julian's time hangs in the chapel of St Luke in Norwich Cathedral today. So Julian was not born in some rustic backwater. She was nurtured in a commercial city of deep religious faith, but also a city at war and in the throes of social change.

Julian the Woman

As Julian tells us nothing about herself and her early life we must piece this together from what we know of the anchoritic life in her era and any personal hints we can glean from her book.

As already stated, the Black Death visited Norwich

three times during Julian's youth. England was at war; taxes were high. Julian's childhood therefore must have been short and sombre. Presuming that she came from the commercial class, her family might have allowed her to help in their trade, whatever it may have been. She would also have learned the usual domestic tasks assigned to women – cooking, managing a household, weaving, carding wool. During the evenings the family would gather round an open fire in the centre of the room and share stories and songs.

At about the age of 15 Julian would need to decide on her future. It used to be assumed that she was a former Benedictine nun as her anchorhold was in the gift of Carrow Priory. Now this is thought unlikely. The Black Death had already depleted religious communities, and in the circumstances Carrow would have been loath to allow one of their number to leave in order to pursue another way of life. Also, there is no mention in her book of anything that would place Julian in a monastic milieu, even had she come from a family that could supply her with a suitable dowry enabling her to take one of the highly desirable places available. She never mentions an abbess or sisters, there is nothing about religious vows, the value of chastity, the recitation of the Divine Office, the Rule. Nor does Julian seem to have been an anchoress at the time of her visions. In the short text she speaks of her mother being in the room (not a Reverend Mother), her parish priest coming accompanied by a boy carrying the cross; the people around her laughing.

Julian is concerned not for monks and nuns but for her fellow Christians, of whom she feels herself to be one. We are on safer ground presuming that Julian married young and perhaps lost her husband (and children?) during the plague or in infancy. Julian is conversant with God as mother most likely through her own experience of motherhood. Also her descriptions of what she sees in her Shewings are drawn from homely metaphors, not a specifically religious environment. She sees the blood of Christ crucified falling and spreading like herrings' scales or rain from the eaves of a house; Jesus is hung out to dry like a cloth left in a cold wind; God wraps us in goodness as a mother swaddles her child.

The faith that Julian speaks of is the faith of the Church as a whole. While there was only one house for nuns in the city, Norwich abounded in monasteries and priories for men. The Benedictines were at the Cathedral. There were Augustinian, Dominican, Franciscan and Carmelite friars engaged in a preaching ministry, and hearing sermons was a popular pastime. Julian could have gleaned her understanding of Church doctrine from such sermons rather than formal study. But while she follows what she considers official teaching she is not afraid to question some aspects of it and draw her own conclusions, such as her refusal to see anyone in hell.

It is likely that Julian became an anchoress only after her near-death experience. As her cell was in the gift of Carrow Priory she may have had a friend or relative there who obtained it for her dwelling when its former occupant died. Other occupants would follow in their turn after Julian's own death.

A woman who wished to lead a life of solitude would have to convince the bishop that she was a worthy candidate, after which the burial service was read over her and she was led to her three-windowed anchorhold for a secluded life of prayer. Anchoresses occasionally taught small children or earned their living by church needlework. Otherwise they relied on people of the locality to provide for their needs by gifts in kind. Clothes were supposed to be plain and warm, but were not considered a religious habit as such. A cat was permitted for keeping down vermin. Cleanliness was highly prized, but not easily maintained in such a small space. A maid would do the necessary outside chores, supply meals and so forth. Julian's days would be busy with prayer and counselling, while the long dark nights gave plenty of time to ponder. It is probable that Julian learned to read and write only after being enclosed, so as to communicate her insights herself, rather than relying on a scribe to take dictation.

Three Requests and Three Wounds

Julian tells us at the beginning of her book of three requests that preceded her serious illness, an illness that brought her to the brink of death and that became the catalyst for her visions or 'Shewings'.

While still young, Julian tells us she had asked God for three things. The first was a vivid perception of Christ's Passion, an experiential knowledge that would involve her emotions and feelings as if she had been present with Our Lady, Mary Magdalen and Christ's other true friends at the crucifixion. To see Christ suffering in the flesh, Julian thought, would enable her to enter more fully into the reality of what had transpired on Calvary. She was obviously, then, a woman who wanted to engage herself fully – mind, heart and body – in the truths of her faith, and for that she was willing and ready to suffer with the suffering Christ, and compassionate with those who were linked to him by ties of the deepest love and friendship.

I thought I had already experienced something of the Passion of Christ, yet by the grace of God I desired to experience still more. I wished I had really been there with Mary Magdalen and the others who loved him and were near him. For this reason I wanted to have a bodily vision through which I could better understand the physical pains of our Lord, together with the compassion of our Lady and all his true lovers alive at the time who saw his pain . . . The reason for this prayer was that I might more truly understand the Passion of Christ.

RDL 2.2

The second request was for the gift of a serious illness to be visited on her when she was 30 years of age.

With regard to the second gift, there came to my mind, with contrition, freely and without seeking it, an intense desire to have from God the gift of a physical illness (at the young age of thirty). I wanted this illness to be severe to the point of death, so that I could receive all the rites of Holy Church, being convinced myself that I should die, and all others seeing me thinking the same . . . I desired this because I wanted to be fully cleansed by the mercy of God, and afterwards, as a result of this illness, live a more consecrated life for the glory of God.

RDL 2.3

Why does Julian specify 30? Possibly because at that age Jesus had traditionally begun his ministry, submitting to being baptized by John after years of preparation in the silence of Nazareth. Julian too, at 30, wants to enter upon a new phase of life thoroughly cleansed by the Last Rites of the Church. In other words, she wants the chance of a new beginning. Possibly, then, we might surmise that in her past there was some sin, some shame, that she wanted to put behind her in a radical manner. The Last Rites would enable her to receive a 'second baptism', as it were, and prepare her to enter upon a new path, a path that would ultimately lead her to embrace the life of an anchoress.

The third request was for the gift of three wounds. This idea had come to her as a result of hearing a sermon about St Cecilia, who reputedly received three neck wounds in the course of her martyrdom (or passion). Julian wants not the physical wounds of the martyr but three interior wounds: the wound of contrition, the wound of compassion, and the wound of longing for God.

> As for the third gift, by the grace of God and the teaching of Holy Church, I developed a strong desire to receive three wounds during my life. That is to say: the wound of true contrition, the wound of natural compassion, and the wound of unshakeable longing for God. And just as I prayed for the other two gifts conditionally, so I prayed for this third one without any condition. The first two desires I soon forgot, but the third remained with me continually.
>
> RDL 2.5

So while Julian tells us she forgot about the first two requests, which she asked for conditionally as being outside the normal run of Christian graces, she kept the request for the three wounds continually in her prayers, asking for them without condition. They were what she really wanted above all else, and she saw them as within the ambience of a normal Christian life. In fact, if we look carefully, they actually include the first two desires, for contrition offers us all a new beginning whenever we turn to God in sorrow; and compassion enables us to enter into the sufferings of others in an empathic manner, whether or not we actually experience something of the passion of Christ in a more vivid way.

The wounds of contrition, compassion and longing are three gifts God wants to give and which we have every right to ask for. For Julian's way, in the end, is not an extraordinary path of visions and revelations, but one that is accessible to all her fellow Christians, and indeed to every person seeking truth.

The fact that God also granted Julian's first two requests was an added bonus. Most of us, however, are not going to receive a near-death experience. Neither will we ever know by means of a vision the reality of Christ's Passion as if we were actually present. But with the wounds of contrition, compassion and longing we can share in the wonder of growing in the knowledge of God and self that is at the heart of Julian's understanding of life.

Why Wounds?

Why did Julian ask for the gift of three wounds rather than just asking straightforwardly for the gifts of contrition, compassion and longing for God? Maybe because there is a long tradition in Scripture that God wounds us in order to heal us.

How happy is the one whom God reproves;
therefore do not despise the discipline of the Almighty.
For he wounds, but he binds up;
he strikes, but his hands heal.

Job 5.17–18

It was through suffering that Israel came to understand the tenderness and fidelity of God towards her despite the people's own infidelity and sinfulness. And in Christian hagiography the wounds of martyrs like Cecilia became their insignia of glory. To those who were not martyrs, the wounds of life itself could become the way in which God's love was communicated to sinners as they came in contact with Christ the healer.

Through wounds, fissures in the self, God finds a way into us that is not possible when we are invulnerable, walled about, safe and secure. Wounds open up areas of the self that we would rather keep hidden. Wounds force us to confront our neediness and pain. But ultimately, for Julian, the wounds of contrition, compassion and longing actually heal us. They enable us to face ourselves, confront our lack, and come through to wholeness and inner peace, knowing that love is the meaning of God and the meaning of life.

The process of conversion is one of transformation, a gradual, generous handing over of the self into the hands of the One who holds us tenderly, yet who is not satisfied with our smallness and lack of capacity. God, as St John of the Cross writes in *The Living Flame of Love*, wounds us out of desire for our growth and fulfilment.

> You have wounded me in order to cure me, O divine hand, and you have put to death in me what made me lifeless, what deprived me of God's life in which I now see myself live . . . And your only begotten Son, O merciful hand of the Father, is the delicate touch by which you touched me with the force of your cautery and wounded me.[1]

The Wounds of Life

Today we are very aware of physical beauty and the desire to preserve and enhance it. Plastic surgery for cosmetic reasons is becoming more common. Creams, lotions, dyes, all help to keep the appearance of ageing at bay. It is a far cry from the biblical world where grey hair entitled one to honour, and there was respect shown to the aged as repositories of wisdom. The elderly were considered valuable inasmuch as they had experienced life and could pass on some of their accumulated life-learning. They were honoured in their ageing, not considered hopelessly 'past their sell-by date' as we might cruelly say now.

As we age, changes take place in us physically as we lose our health and strength and ability to perform. But in our bodies is embedded the story of our life – our actions, our illnesses, our weaknesses, our choices for good and evil, our scars from childbirth and operations, our chapped hands, our thinning hair, our wrinkles and laughter lines. These show outwardly what we are within.

> My deeds will be measured not by my youthful
>   appearance,
> but by the concern lines on my forehead,
> the laugh lines around my mouth,
> and the chins from seeing what can be done
> for those smaller than me who have fallen.

> Erma Bombeck

We have written into our bodies the story of our individual life and what we have made of it. These are our 'wounds', the outward manifestation of the ways we have grown and changed. They reveal the inroads that life has made into our being. They are not to be disguised, nor are they reason to be ashamed. Not one of us reaches adulthood, and certainly not old age, without some physical and psychological scarring. Julian calls our wounds, like the wounds of Christ, 'honourable scars'. They show us who we have become, the lessons that life has taught us, the sins, the virtues, the whole gamut of our individual personality, for we are indeed a 'marvellous mixture of good and bad', as Julian says, and can learn from all that has happened to us and all that we have chosen to do with our life for good or ill.

The human person physically, emotionally, psychologically, spiritually, is a wounded person, yet one striving towards wholeness, one who is totally unique. No other person has exactly the same scars and wrinkles (whether inner or outer) as I have. And it is often our very woundedness that enables us to be compassionate and understanding to those who struggle.

Caryll Houselander (1901–54) was another English mystic who, like Julian, was attuned to the inner world of herself and others. She exhibited an enormous capacity for empathy because of her own emotional fragility, a fragility that originated with the divorce of her parents and various psychosomatic illnesses that dogged her early childhood. With this background she seemed able to enter empathically into the vulnerable hearts of the wounded and psychologically unbalanced persons who came to her, sometimes sent by professionals, sometimes coming of their own accord, sensing a kindred soul who would understand and not judge them.

It was Caryll's ability to embrace her own woundedness that made her a channel of healing. She was an artist and writer of originality and depth, drawing creative strength from her experience and sharing it with others.

One of the sorrows of Caryll's life was that she never married, although she had many really good friends and made her home with one of them, a divorced woman, whose daughter she helped to raise. The man she had loved passionately married someone else and Caryll had to let him go. He died later in Russia and she never saw him again.

During the Second World War, Caryll met the poet Stephen Spender's sister, Christine, who also aspired to be a writer (as Caryll was herself). They corresponded for some time, during which Christine confided to Caryll her own heartbreak at having to renounce the man she loved as he was not free to marry her. In a letter of reply Caryll encourages Christine to talk to a priest she knows and not try to keep everything to herself. She writes:

> Never mind about showing ugly things; a real healer is like a doctor, who doesn't see a sore as ugly once he has put balm on it, because he is only interested in seeing the healing process on it. Remember . . . that it is at the sore place, and only there, that our healing begins; and that, whenever healing does begin at a sore which you have had the courage and love to expose, there, in that sore spot, the healing of the whole world begins . . .[2]

Earlier Caryll had written to the same woman:

> Here I can only pray for you. I know what it feels like to part from a man whom one is in love with, for I have done so too, many years ago – and the years have not lessened or dimmed the love, even though he is dead

now . . . I know what an anguish such a parting can be, but tell you, in case you can find any ray of comfort for yourself in it, that certainly in my case it hasn't brought any sense of waste or frustration, but a kind of richness and completeness that nothing else could have . . . Also . . . because I loved that man, I have loved many other people, animals and things. Perhaps later on you too will have these comforts.[3]

Caryll does not deny the wound, but she also acknowledges how it has increased her capacity in other areas. The experience of life and love has not been wasted, even if, in this case, it has remained unfulfilled on the physical level.

Wounded for Purpose

Henri Nouwen, another person who helped countless others, acknowledged that his own particular wound – the excessive desire and need for affection – would remain with him permanently. Yet it was responsible for much of his own giftedness, manifested in a unique ability to touch others in their own pain through his books and talks.

What to do with this inner wound that is so easily touched and starts bleeding again? It is such a familiar wound. It has been with me for many years. I don't think this wound – this immense need for affection, and this immense fear of rejection – will ever go away. It is there to stay, but maybe for a good reason. Perhaps it is a gateway to my salvation, a door to glory, and a passage to freedom.[4]

[29]

So in asking for wounds Julian is asking in some way for an increase in her capacity for contrition, for compassion and for longing. Painful as it may be to grow in these gifts, they will ultimately make inroads into her being that will open her more deeply to life, to love and to God. God is a God of life and peace, not destruction and pain.

Julian may be a wounded woman, one who has known tragedy, diminishment, sin. But she knows too that in the end 'all will be well' for God is greater than our own petty thinking, and God embraces us as we are, not as we think we ought to be or would like to be.

In his book on the spiritual tradition of the desert, Alan Jones writes of visiting an Egyptian monastery where his monastic guide gives him three gifts: a small bouquet of flowers and herbs, symbolic of beauty; a simple yet wholesome meal to assuage bodily hunger; and three vials of oil. The oil is offered with the words, 'Take these, brother, for your wounds and for the healing of others' hurts. We all need the saving and healing power of Christ.'⁵ So we do. Each of us is wounded, each of us is in need of healing. And we are in this together.

Space to Reflect

Christ also suffered for you, leaving you an example, so that you should follow in his steps . . . He himself bore our sins in his body on the cross, so that, free from sins, we might live for righteousness; by his wounds you have been healed.

1 Peter 2.21, 24

Wounded People

The fact that Jesus suffered as we do is one of the ways in which we relate to his humanity, being 'one like us' in all things but sin. None of us goes through life without suffering psychological and emotional wounds of some kind.

Look back on your life up to this point and name one wound belonging to your childhood, one to your adolescence, one to your adulthood. No doubt you can easily think of many more. Often we think that we would be better if we were more 'whole' persons. Yet there is a sense in which our wounds are so much part of who we are that without them we would not be complete.

Think now of how your wounds have opened you up to areas of life that otherwise would have been closed to you and name some of them. For example, the wound of rejection as a young child may have made you more sensitive to other such children; more understanding when adults who have experienced rejection seem to be over-demanding in their need for affection.

Moving On

Julian never spends her time in self-pity or recriminations over the past. She is always ready to point to God and God's goodness, knowing that it is more powerful than any evil we can do. The spate of books that have come out recently in which men and women have shared with their readers how they have endured the most horrific childhood abuse, end in celebrating the ultimate triumph of the human spirit. Our tendency is to stop at our wounds. Julian and the saints teach us to go beyond them. We do not have to explain them. We have to accept, learn, forgive and move on. Julian writes:

It seems to me that pain is something real, and it lasts for a while, purifying us and making us know ourselves so that we ask for mercy. But the Passion of Christ is a comfort to us in all this, and this is his blessed will. Because of the tender love that our Lord has for those who shall be saved, he gives comfort quickly and sweetly, as if he said 'Yes, it is true, sin is the cause of all pain; but all shall be well, and all shall be well, and all manner of things shall be well.'

RDL 27.5

Spend some time silently pondering these famous words of Julian, 'All shall be well . . .', and think how they might apply to your own life right now.

St John of the Cross

John of the Cross (1542–91) was the youngest child of parents who had faced social rejection because of their love for each other. After his father died when John was still an infant, the mother was left penniless with three boys to bring up. The middle boy soon died of malnutrition, for his mother could barely support the family despite doing piece work as a weaver. John also had to work from an early age, ending up as a teenage nurse in a hospital for those suffering from venereal diseases. Even when he became a friar, John's brothers in the Order persecuted and disliked him. He was imprisoned, whipped, starved, and only just escaped with his life. Yet from this little man, prematurely bald and stunted in growth, flowed the most beautiful love poetry. In his poems he made sense of his suffering, seeing it as a gift from God, and inviting him to a deeper self-offering. No wonder he became known as a sensitive and compassionate spiritual director. In one of his books, *The Living Flame of Love*, he writes these words:

There is here a great paradox. The more we are wounded the more healthy we are. For the continued burning of love's fire both heals and soothes even while it inflicts pain. Indeed, the wounding is only present so that the Spirit may comfort us more deeply and more abundantly.

Scriptural Meditation

The thought of my affliction and homelessness is wormwood and gall! My soul continually thinks of it and is bowed down within me. But this I call to mind, and therefore I have hope: The steadfast love of the Lord never ceases, his mercies never come to an end; they are new every morning; great is your faithfulness.

Lamentations 3.19–23

Prayer

O sweet burn!
O delicious wound!
O tender hand!
O gentle touch!
Savouring of everlasting life
And paying the whole debt.
In destroying death you have changed it into life.

St John of the Cross

Notes

1 John of the Cross, St, *The Living Flame of Love*, in *Collected Works*, trans. K. Kavanaugh and O. Rodriguez, ICS Publications, 1991, p. 664.
2 Letter to Christine Spender, in Houselander, C., *The Letters of Caryll Houselander*, ed. M. Ward, Sheed & Ward, 1973, p. 110.
3 Houselander, *Letters*, p. 108.
4 Nouwen, H., *Sabbatical Journey*, quoted in O'Laughlin, M., *Henri Nouwen: His Life and Vision*, Orbis Books, 2005, p. 159.
5 Jones, A., *Soul Making: The Desert Way of Spirituality*, SCM Press, 1986, p. 15.

3

Julian's Window on to Everyday Life and the Wound of Contrition

*I*t is noteworthy that Julian prefixes the request for each wound with a qualifying adjective. She asks for *true* contrition, *natural* compassion and *unshakeable* longing for God.

So what might be involved in true contrition? Surely not any kind of overpowering and immobilizing guilt or self-hatred. Julian does not teach us to berate ourselves, but to see ourselves as we are in the sight of God's grace and mercy – children accepted and loved.

True contrition is not a violent affair. Spiritual writers link it with the gift of tears, a manifestation of compunction, or piercing of the heart. Tears well up from the depths of our being when we are confronted with who we are in truth, and who the God is who offers us new life. Tears are, as it were, a second baptism, clearing our vision, cleansing our heart. 'They are like the breaking of the waters of the womb before the birth of a child.'[1]

Biblical Foundations

In the Scriptures, repentance – another name for contrition – comes from the Hebrew word *teshuva*, which means 'return'. To return to God is to return also to oneself, and to be received by One who accepts and forgives.

> Return, O Israel, to the Lord your God,
> for you have stumbled because of your iniquity . . .
> I will heal their disloyalty;
> I will love them freely . . .
> They shall again live beneath my shadow,
> they shall flourish as a garden;
> they shall blossom like the vine,
> their fragrance shall be like the wine of Lebanon.
>
> Hosea 14.1, 4, 7

> Return, faithless Israel, says the Lord.
> I will not look on you in anger,
> for I am merciful.
>
> Jeremiah 3.11b

After testing Israel God will always take her back because God loves her and continually calls her home to herself, to her true vocation, and to God.

> Thus says the Lord:
> 'The people who survived the sword
> found grace in the wilderness;
> when Israel sought for rest,
> the Lord appeared to him from far away.
> I have loved you with an everlasting love;
> therefore I have continued my faithfulness to you.

Again I will build you, and you shall be built,
O virgin Israel! ...
For there shall be a day when sentinels will call
in the hill country of Ephraim:
"Come, let us go up to Zion,
to the Lord our God."'

Jeremiah 31.2–6

When Jesus speaks in the Gospels of repentance he means this return that has the marks of complete forgiveness, total acceptance, and the wonder of God's fidelity to those who stray. It is mirrored in the parables, which tell of the return of the prodigal, the finding and bringing home of the lost sheep, the discovery of the lost coin. In the last analysis repentance is joy, because it means coming back to the arms of the living God who awaits us.

The rabbis identified three stages of *teshuva*: the admission of having done wrong; sorrow for the offence; resolution not to repeat the sin. The gates of repentance are always open to the one who returns. Martin Buber takes this concept a stage further in a way that ties in with Julian. *Teshuva* is the turning of the total person towards God. Sin is lack of integrity, a symbol of the divided self. In turning to God the sinner finds God turning towards him or her in an I–Thou relationship of love and friendship. We once more 'behold the face of God' and can reflect it to others as whole persons.

Contrition as Knowing Self and Knowing God

And so I saw with absolute certainty that it is easier and quicker for us to know God than it is to know our own

[37]

soul. For our soul is so deeply grounded in God, and so endlessly treasured, that we cannot come to know it until we first know God its creator, to whom it is united. Nevertheless, I saw that in order to reach natural maturity we must have a wise and sincere desire to know our own soul, whereby we are taught to seek it where it is to be found – that is, in God. So by the leading of the Holy Spirit through grace, we shall know both in one. It does not matter whether we are moved to know God or our soul, both desires are good and true.

RDL 56.1

Knowledge of self and knowledge of God go hand in hand. But as in the scriptural picture of God this is not a knowledge that casts us down in despair. It is a knowledge that enables us to relax and be who we are without disguise. Perhaps we could call it by the old-fashioned name of humility, a name deriving from the Latin *humus*, soil. Self-knowledge roots us in reality, 'grounds us' as Julian would say, in true self-acceptance. We are creatures loved and redeemed, not over-inflated actors strutting across the human stage in the mistaken belief that all eyes are riveted on our performance, playing to the gallery of other peoples' opinions, and fearing that if we fail then all is lost. That is slavery, according to Teresa of Avila, not freedom, for 'humility is truth' and we cannot be relaxed or content if we live with lies and pretence.

Humility is ready to acknowledge that the world does not revolve around us and our own needs, hopes and plans. Others do not have to measure up to our ideas of 'perfection'. We stop trying to control everything and everyone else, confident that we are loved and accepted, not because we are good but because God is good. It is all

[38]

right not to be perfect, to recognize that we fail and sin as did Israel of old, that we have wasted opportunities for doing and being what God wants us to do and be. Did not Jesus say that he came to call sinners rather than the just?

There is no hint in the Gospels that Jesus makes sinners feel bad about themselves. He sees their potential for good despite their woundedness. Sinners make up the human race and we are all sinners.

Jean Sulivan encapsulates this idea in his novel *Eternity, My Beloved*, putting these words into the mouth of the priest Strozzi:

If streetwalkers precede us into the kingdom, it's not because the Son of Man is giving them a reward but verifying a fact. The prostitute is more truthful, more authentic, than most of us because of the knowledge and consciousness she has of her wretched situation; because she is more capable of humility. On the other hand, there's no end to the prostitution of the highly placed; they go on pretending, issuing statements, organizing justice, charity, morality, even the love of God, for their own profit. It's all done so skillfully that it takes a miracle, the greatest of all miracles, for a righteous person to awaken to the realization of their own wrongdoing and iniquity.[2]

Contrition is a wound because self-knowledge can be painful and joyful at the same time. It lances the boil of our pretentiousness. It lets the poison of self-righteousness flow out, exposing the sore to the air of truth, enabling God to enfold us in tenderness, taking our poverty and need to the Divine Heart.

Most of us have to work at being genuine, letting our

masks drop, allowing others, and above all ourselves, to see ourselves just as we are; yet recognizing our greatness as God's beloved children, each one unique and irreplaceable.

Humility is making ourselves available to God as Mary did, knowing herself to be frail and limited, wholly subject to God – a God who loves and chooses whoever God wishes. It is in beholding the Creator that we are filled with true humility, rather than concentrating on ourselves and our lack of virtue.

> For of all things, the beholding and loving of the Creator makes the soul seem less in its own eyes, and fills it fully with reverent fear, true humility, and abundant love for all fellow-Christians.
>
> In order to teach us these things (as far as I can see) our good Lord showed me ... our Lady St Mary, namely the exalted wisdom and truth which were hers as she contemplated her Creator. It was this wisdom and truth that enabled her to contemplate her God who is so great, so high, so mighty and so good. The greatness and nobility of her vision of God filled her with a reverent fear, enabling her to see herself as so little, so lowly, so simple and so poor compared to her Lord. This reverent fear in turn filled her with humility; and so, because of this she was filled with grace and with every kind of virtue.

RDL 6.7–7.1

A rabbinic tale tells of Rabbi Zuzya saying that at the gates of heaven he will not be asked, 'Why were you not Moses?' but 'Why were you not Zuzya?' God will not ask us why we were not Mary, but why did we not respond to life and to God as our unique self. God knows us by name. God calls us as we are. Knowing this God who calls and knowing ourselves as called are two sides of the same coin.

Humility is to have place
deep in the secret of God's face

where one can know, past all surmise,
that God's great will alone is wise,

where one is loved, where one can trust
a strength not circumscribed by dust.

It is to have a place to hide
when all is hurricane outside.[3]

Contrition as Conversion

Coming to self-knowledge means reaching the point of conversion, touching the springs within from which life can flow.

Now one of the things that blocks genuine conversion is a wrong sense of guilt. Often in the past certain schemes of humility were proposed, intended to cultivate an ideal of the humble person. Certain ways of behaving, of speaking, of walking, were superimposed on the person, who was trained in a variety of 'humble' responses. Inability to conform led to profound feelings of guilt and shame. But inappropriate guilt feelings cause a paralysis of the person; they constrict the flow of life in us because everything is concerned with our own deeds and our own efforts. The desire to please, to seem spiritual, to reach an abstract 'perfection' has nothing to do with real conversion.

Conversion means contacting our real depths and our real desires. So often today the therapist is the person who enables someone to reach this kind of freedom rather than the official minister of religion, because in a therapeutic relationship the deepest areas of the person are allowed to surface without judgement.

Conversion enables the grace of God to be inserted into the point of our weakness. The Cistercian abbot André Louf, who is both priest and psychotherapist, has put his finger on a number of truths in this regard, for he has brought to spiritual accompaniment not only the wisdom of monastic tradition but also the insights of modern psychology. He writes:

[False] humility is a clumsy expression of indefinite feelings of guilt, but it does not leave in the heart a single trace of genuine humility. False humility tends rather to impose restraints on the heart and paralyse it because, with all the tricks at its disposal, it causes one to evade the truth that could trigger the awareness of one's real sin. But these days, the reaction to this guilt feeling is often to adopt a sort of false freedom which crowds out the confrontation with sin and represses any upsurge of repentance. In both cases the unconscious attempt is to the same purpose – to escape the feeling of falling short and of being a sinner.

The alternative to false guilt and false freedom can only be overcome in genuine evangelical repentance, that is, in the brokenness of heart that is purely a gift of the Holy Spirit. Through that process alone a person may arrive at full truth in his or her relationship to God and in the end, to genuine love; for love alone is the foundation of true freedom.[4]

Because the old forms of humility based on inculcating feelings of false guilt have not proved life giving, there is a move now towards banishing all moral norms. But this is not what Scripture proclaims. God loves us sinners with a love that reaches right down to our subconscious depths. God has nothing to do with the super-ego and its grandiose claims to 'goodness'.

It is only when anxiety, shame and guilt feelings have been allowed to surface and been looked at dispassionately, with a companion to witness our faltering words as we search our inmost hearts, that real sin can come to light. And sin often turns out to be where we least expected it.

However, we will not expose ourselves unless we know we are loved, and a companionship of love makes us vulnerable. If we love we have the capacity to wound and be wounded. But if love is offered and worked with and through, then the springs of the waters of life within us can be set free to well up of their own accord.

Conversion means facing the truth and trusting in both mercy and grace – forgiveness and healing. Julian is our guide to holding these two in tension. Mercy is present in her absolute prohibition of judging, so that we may feel free to expose in confidence who we really are and be met in our place of weakness by 'tender eyes'. We are assured by Julian that there is no anger in a God who, whatever we may have done, continues to regard us with the gaze of a kind and merciful friend.

Grace, by contrast, gives us courage and strength to rise up, to grasp our destiny and dignity, to affirm the greatness of our calling. Conversion implies the strength and confidence that are born of joy, the joy of being open to God and others without cringing or hiding.

Mercy is a property full of compassion, which belongs to motherhood in tender love.

Grace is a property full of glory which belongs to royal lordship in the same love.

Mercy works thus: protecting, enduring, bringing life and healing; and all is from the tenderness of love.

Grace works with mercy: bringing up, rewarding, endlessly exceeding everything that our love and labour deserve, spreading forth widely and showing the noble and abundant generosity of our Lord's royal lordship in his marvellous courtesy. And this is from the abundance of love.

For grace transforms our dreadful failing into plentiful and endless consolation.

And grace transforms our shameful falling into high and glorious rising.

And grace transforms our sorrowful dying into holy and blissful life.

RDL 48.4

So often people in the past were aware of sinfulness and not sufficiently aware of mercy and grace. To Julian we are basically good, so there is no need to be anxious about salvation. God is a God of peace, and peace flows from the core of a person who is in touch with the true self. At that point real conversion begins, enabling us to be who we are and become who we are called to be.

Solitude – the Path to Self-Knowledge

Julian lived much of her life in a single cell attached to St Julian's Church. She had to learn to live with herself, to get to know herself and love her own company. This is a discipline that is indispensible. How is it that we are willing to inflict our company on others for many hours of each day, yet cannot remain in our own company for even half an hour without seeking distraction!

Over-activity, stress, the inability to say no or to remain in quiet without music or books to crowd out the silence, are inimical to spiritual growth. Activism keeps us from facing ourselves, for at some level we fear what we may find. Hence the diffused anxiety, the filling of every moment with some duty, even spiritual duties like formal prayer.

Learning to be silent makes it possible to live peacefully with ourselves, for until we can do that we will communicate our own inner restlessness to the people we meet.

It seems that those who have embraced solitude and remained faithful to it have learned to accept themselves at a very deep level. Having encountered their loneliness and incompleteness they have reached a place where poverty, inner and outer, fosters transparency of soul. They have nothing to lose.

In his travels through the Middle East, William Dalrymple tells of visiting the Coptic monastery of St Anthony in Egypt. There one of the monks tells Dalrymple of his struggle to live poorly and without distraction in prayer. The writer counters with the remark that surely one doesn't have to go into the desert to find an empty room free of distractions, this can surely be found too in any city – Cairo, Alexandria, London . . . The dialogue continues as follows:

'What you say is true,' said Fr Dioscuros with a smile. 'You can pray anywhere. After all, God is everywhere, so you can find him everywhere.' He gestured to the darkening sand dunes outside: 'But in the desert, in the pure, clean atmosphere, in the silence – there you can find yourself. And unless you begin to know yourself, how can you even begin to search for God.'[5]

Without some element of solitude we keep ourselves at bay, as it were. In solitude we are forced to confront our inner anguish and pain. Yet these are what God wants to take upon Godself in Christ. The facts are friendly, but we need to face those facts – the fact of our incompleteness, our woundedness, our hidden agendas. In solitude there is no one to see us, no one to applaud or condemn – only ourselves.

Those who enter on a spiritual path today and embrace a modicum of silence and solitude often find themselves in need of professional counselling to cope with the emergence of suppressed memories that have caused personal hurt and damage. The dysfunctional family, the abusive relationships, the inner confusion begin to surface. This is a sign that solitude is beginning to do its work, not a sign that things have gone wrong.

Those experiences that bring about a true facing of the self are blessings. Not all are called to the solitude of the cell as Julian was, but all are invited to the self-knowledge that the cell symbolizes. It is the place where one works upon one's inner being, first with difficulty and pain, later with joyful acceptance of one's poverty, fully dependent upon a God who is love.

The God Julian speaks of is like a tender mother, who enables growth to take place at the right time, not expect-

ing too much too soon. Thus the preliminary pain of
silence and solitude becomes a joy. I grow in trust,
acknowledging my uniqueness as a child of God, with my
own particular history, my own particular journey, my
own birth process.

> In the case of our spiritual birth [Jesus] looks after us
> with a tenderness that is far beyond comparison,
> because our soul is so much more precious in his sight.
> He fires our understanding, he directs our way, he
> soothes our conscience, he comforts our soul, he illu-
> mines our heart . . . He enables us to love everything he
> loves out of love for him, and to be thoroughly satisfied
> with him and all his works. When we fall he quickly lifts
> us up with a loving embrace of love and the touch of his
> grace. When we have been strengthened by all this
> sweet work that he does in us then, helped by his grace,
> we choose with all our will to be his servants and his
> lovers for ever unending.

RDL 61.1

One wonders about the background that must have
allowed Julian to live as an anchoress. What was her home
life like? Her family? Did she have children of her own?
What were her thoughts as she wrestled with her particular weaknesses and sins? What we can be sure of amid all
the speculation is that she understood in the long term
that the answer was to trust in a God who accepted her
with the unconditional love that a good mother knows for
her own child, come what may.

The two sins that are the most dangerous in Julian's
eyes are sloth and despair; nothing to do with sex or
evil actions. Sloth means putting off the moment of

conversion, resisting growth. Keeping ourselves 'busy' can actually be a form of laziness, by which we circumvent the inner work we have to do and remain on the surface of life instead. We have to 'take time' for self, for God, for relationships that nourish us, and work at these things. Sloth also includes resistance to suffering. We do not want the radical demands that God and life make on us, so we find ways to evade and avoid them. Sloth undermines belief in our potential, and makes us satisfied with the line of least resistance. We cease to do good because it is all too much trouble to bestir ourselves.

Despair means losing hope, feeling that it is all too late to do anything better with our life. It makes us sink down into a greater laziness with an attitude of 'what's the use?' Indeed, when we see ourselves so weak we wonder whether it is worth going on the spiritual journey at all.

To acknowledge depression, weakness, blindness, frailty, is not the problem. That is part of being human. God does not allow any of this to be wasted. Our part is to trust that we are indeed 'kept securely'. Courage is but another name for going on when we feel like giving up.

The Problem of Sin

There is no getting away from Julian's preoccupation with the problem of sin. If there is no sin there is no need for contrition. As we are one in the love of God, so we are linked in solidarity by our sinfulness. The crucifixion is the revelation of the love and pain that God takes upon Godself because of the sin that has caused a fracture in the human being. Sin is the cause of suffering and needs to be addressed.

Often we do not like to think of ourselves as sinners; yet we are willing to accept that we are wounded, broken people, who have contributed to the wounding and breaking of the world, either inadvertently or by deliberate choice. That is why silence and solitude are hard for us. They make us conscious not only of our own brokenness but also of the pain we have caused others.

Julian wrestles, as we all do, with the meaning of sin and evil. She is also concerned with the question of whether sin can be constructive in our lives, or whether it is always destructive. In this context we have her most famous phrase that 'All shall be well, and all shall be well and all manner of things shall be well', and her insight that in God there is no anger. God is always 'on our side', as it were, when we struggle. God is not there to condemn or punish but to bring good out of everything.

In Chapter 11 of her *Revelations* Julian sees God in a point. As this single point symbolizes God, she wonders how there can be any room for sin. Note that here she is looking at the question from God's side, not from the side of human actions. Here she sees that sin is a lack of goodness, not something positive at all. Later Julian will look more deeply at the vileness of sin, but she is adamant that it is in our nature to hate sin. We are naturally drawn to the good, even though we know well that we have done wrong, or 'missed the mark' as the Hebrew word for sin, *het*, indicates.

While sin will always remain a mystery, the greatest comfort is that sin can be turned to good. In fact, there are things we learn through our sins and mistakes that we could never learn otherwise. How true it is that we never really learn from the mistakes of others, only our own! God's love for us 'cannot and will not be broken by sin', says Julian (*RDL* 61.2). God allows us to fall in order to break through our self-righteousness and inculcate an attitude of tenderness and understanding towards others.

Julian looks at examples from Scripture and the saints: David; Peter; Mary Magdalene; St John of Beverly (*RDL* 38.2). Yes, they sinned but their sin was integrated into their whole life experience and became a cause for rejoicing at God's mercy. Indeed their woundedness has become in heaven a sign of glory, just as Jesus himself still bears his glorified wounds. God never lets us go, and so we must never let go of God by turning away on account of our wrongdoing.

> Our good Lord protects us most tenderly when it seems to us that we are almost forsaken and cast off because of our sins, and because we see that this is well deserved. Yet because of the humility that we learn from this we are raised very high in God's sight by his grace. Furthermore, through the special graces of increased contrition, compassion and longing for the will of God, God invites those he chooses in such a way that they are suddenly delivered from sin and pain and taken up to bliss, being made equal with the saints.
>
> By contrition we are made clean.
>
> By compassion we are made ready.
>
> By true longing for God we are made worthy.
>
> These are the three means (as I see it) by which all souls get to heaven – that is to say, those who were sinners on earth and are destined to be saved.
>
> For every sinful soul must be healed by these medicines. Yet even though the sinner is healed, the wounds are still seen by God, not now as wounds but rather as

signs of honour. And so we see things turned upside down.

RDL 39.2–3

Julian allows us the dignity of responsibility. She does not minimize our sinfulness. She does not tell us that we have always done the best thing or the right thing. That would be to collude in wilful blindness. Yet she holds out hope, not just of forgiveness but of things being even better than when we lived in innocence and ignorance. We can be grown up, responsible persons, for whom God turns all things to good. It is through a restored innocence, not one that has never faced the darkness, that Christ is encountered.

I questioned innocence renewed by grace:
what did you see on hills beatified?
What voices heard you in the holy place?
With words of light the penitent replied:

Under the night's impenetrable cover
wherein I walked beset by many fears,
I saw the radiant face of Christ the Lover,
and it was wet with tears.[6]

The First Window

I see the wound of contrition as corresponding to the first window in Julian's cell, the window that communicates with the servant and which, when fully opened, gives Julian access to the garden, the churchyard and the world of nature.

This window symbolizes our common humanity, our sharing in the created world of beauty and pain, our need to serve and be served in a community of equals, where we are all one before God.

It is also the door for Julian's cat to go in and out, foraging and prowling around as animals do. It is the most natural window open to the give and take of all life with its bodily necessities of food, drink, clothing, excretion.

We know that during her stay in the anchorhold Julian had at least two servants, Alice and Sarah, for they are mentioned in wills. She needed others, as we all do, in order to survive. And through her relationship with Alice and Sarah, as much as with God, Julian was asked to grow in self-knowledge, self-acceptance and friendship.

Through the diligence of her maids Julian had to trust that she would be provided for and receive what she needed from 'outside'. Solitude is always relative. It does not remove us from the human community but enables us to live in it from the humble place of a wounded humanity that is not sufficient of itself.

Space to Reflect

I tell you, there will be more joy in heaven over one sinner who repents than over ninety-nine righteous people who need no repentance.

Luke 15.7

I tell you, her sins, which were many, have been forgiven; hence she has shown great love. But the one to whom little is forgiven loves little.

Luke 7.47–48

Self-Knowledge and Self-Acceptance

One of the things we find hard is to really accept who we are. Either we put ourselves down, or we justify the most outrageous behaviour, even actions that cause real hurt to others, because we 'want to be ourselves' at any price. We are not willing to take responsibility. Either we blame others and excuse ourselves, or we harshly condemn even the most innocent of actions. Acceptance of self means a readiness to be real – in our own eyes and in the eyes of others who love us.

Can you think of someone who, because they loved you, saw the best in you and thus managed to bring it to the surface? In the Gospels, joy is always the result of genuine repentance and self-knowledge, and it causes us to offer forgiveness and mercy in our turn to those whose lives are spoiled and soiled. It is to spread joy in the same way that God offers us the joy of a new beginning whenever we wish.

Make a resolution to offer someone this joy today.

Saints and Sinners

The Scriptures are full of real people, all a mixture of good and bad. Julian sees this as the human condition, it is unavoidable. Yet it is through their failings and sins that the saints came to a deeper self-knowledge and greater compassion for others. Julian writes of St John of Beverly as follows, though the sins she is referring to are not specified.

St John of Beverley was shown by our Lord for our comfort as both very exalted and very ordinary. The Lord brought to my mind how St John of Beverley is one of our own dear countrymen, known to us all. God called him simply 'St John of Beverley' just as we do. He did this with an expression full of joy and sweetness . . . With this God reminded me that in his youth and tender years he was a beloved servant of God who greatly loved and feared him. Nevertheless, God allowed him to fall into sin, while mercifully protecting him so that he did not perish or lose any time, and afterwards God raised him to a much higher and manifold grace. And because of the deep repentance and humility he had in his life, God has given him many joys in heaven – joys which far exceed what he would have had if he had never sinned or fallen.

RDL 38.4

Think back on your own life. What have you learned through your sins that you could never have known otherwise? Is it possible to be always 'safe', or is risking failure part of growing up to be one's own person?

St Teresa of Avila

St Teresa of Avila (1515–82) was a contemporary of John of the Cross. But unlike him she came from an aristocratic family where everything she wanted was provided for her. When Teresa entered the Carmelite convent in Avila at the age of 21 she continued to live a divided life – given neither wholly to God nor to the world. As she vacillated from year to year, she went one day into a room where there was an image of Christ scourged at the pillar. Suddenly she was overwhelmed with sorrow for her sins and resolved to turn wholeheartedly to God. From that time forward she began to change, and eventually became the great reformer of her Order. But it was the experience of her weaknesses that enabled her to legislate wisely, so that those who followed her could avoid some of her own mistakes. Teresa's strength of will, her humour, her natural and spiritual giftedness in many areas, make her one of the most attractive and human of saints. The memory of her past unfaithfulness never held her back, but became a spur to ever greater self-giving.

Spiritual Meditation

I will sprinkle clean water upon you, and you shall be clean from all your uncleannesses, and from all your idols I will cleanse you. A new heart I will give you, and a new spirit I will put within you; and I will remove from your body the heart of stone and give you a heart of flesh.

Ezekiel 36.25–26

Prayer

Do you strengthen and prepare my soul first of all,
good of all good my Jesus,
and then ordain means whereby I may do something
    for you.
For no one could bear to receive as much as I have done
and pay nothing in return.
Here is my life, my honour, my will, I am yours,
dispose of me according to your desire.
I know well how little I am capable of,
but I shall be able to do all
provided that you withdraw not yourself from me.

St Teresa of Avila

Notes

1 Jones, A., *Soul Making: The Desert Way of Spirituality*, SCM Press, 1986, p. 85.
2 Sulivan, J., *Eternity, My Beloved*, trans. Sr F. E. O'Riordan, River Boat Books, 1999, p. 92.
3 From the poem 'Humility', by Jessica Powers, in Powers, J., *Selected Poetry*, ed. R. Siegfried and R. Morneau, Sheed & Ward, 1989, p. 92.
4 Louf, A., *Tuning into Grace*, DLT, 1992, p. 60.
5 Dalrymple, W., *From the Holy Mountain*, HarperCollins, 1998, p. 410.
6 From the poem 'The Mountains of the Lord', by Jessica Powers, in Powers, *Selected Poetry*, p. 8.

4

Julian's Window of Welcome and the Wound of Compassion

*J*ulian qualifies her request for the second wound with the word 'kind' or natural. She wants that quality of compassion that belongs to our humanity at its best, and reflects the same quality found in God.

Biblical Foundations

The Hebrew Scriptures show God as a God of compassion, a God who forgives, who renews, who offers understanding of us in our weakness, a God who enables us to start over.

> The Lord passed before [Moses] and proclaimed, 'The Lord, the Lord, a God merciful and gracious, slow to anger, and abounding in steadfast love and faithfulness.'
>
> Exodus 34.6

> Bless the Lord, O my soul,
> and all that is within me, bless his holy name.
> Bless the Lord, O my soul,

and do not forget all his benefits –
who forgives all your iniquity,
who heals all your diseases,
who redeems your life from the Pit,
who crowns you with steadfast love and mercy.

Psalm 103.1–4

The Hebrew word for mercy or compassion is *hesed*, meaning 'loving kindness'. It is a divine quality to be reflected in the mercy the Jewish people are called to show others, remembering always that they were redeemed from slavery by a God who had loved and chosen them without any merit on their part (Deuteronomy 7.7).

Hesed is often linked with the Hebrew word *emet* (faith). Together they signify God's utter dependability, his unchanging, faithful love. God has compassion on faithless Israel. God offers forgiveness and mercy at every turn. So must we. It is part of being God's people. We are called to love as God loves, to forgive as God forgives, to be compassionate as God is compassionate.

Above all, the faithful love of God is shown in the gift of Jesus, who in his passion and death demonstrates beyond doubt that his own love for us sinners is sure and dependable even in the face of torture and death.

Julian and Compassion

As Julian lies dying at the age of 30, and the priest brings the crucifix to her room, she looks at it and asks for the second wound – the wound of compassion. It is the wound that enables her to understand from within the sufferings of the wounded and crucified Christ.

Then it suddenly came to my mind that I should ask for the second wound of our Lord's gracious gift, that my body might be filled with the memory and feeling of his blessed Passion, as I had prayed for before. I wanted his pains to be my pains, to feel so deeply with him that I would long for God. In this way I thought I could, by his grace, have the wounds which I had previously desired.

RDL 3.5

At this point God grants her desire, not just for the second wound but also for a vision, the gift Julian had prayed for so many years ago, the gift of experiencing the passion of Jesus as if she had actually been present. This would imprint his sufferings on her mind and heart in a very deep and visual manner. Similarly, Mel Gibson's film *The Passion of the Christ*, in its vivid depiction of the sufferings of Jesus, made viewers aware in a completely new way of all that Jesus had suffered. And not only what Jesus suffered, women identified with the sufferings of his mother as well. It is one thing to read about the Cross, another to 'see' it and realize the price paid for our redemption.

But while Julian certainly 'sees' the pains of Jesus, she moves beyond them to their deeper meaning. Some of Julian's favourite words are homeliness, friendliness, courtesy. The crucifixion is the supreme proof of God's friendship, for only a friend could expose himself in such radical nakedness as Jesus does on the cross. And for one who loves and suffers and proves himself friend beyond doubt, the only proper response is to 'choose Jesus' to be one's heaven (*RDL* 19.2), and long to be like him.

Compassion as Empathic Love

As Julian looks at the suffering Christ her thoughts turn
to Mary who must watch her son being crucified. To be
compassionate is to share in the passion of another
through empathic love. A mother who must watch her
child suffer would rather bear the pain herself. But she
cannot. She can only 'be there' and 'be with'.

From looking at Jesus and Mary, Julian moves away
from being concerned with her personal feelings of sorrow
to include all her fellow Christians, for we are all one
in Christ's body, the Church. The passion reveals how
Jesus loves us, and how he, in his turn, is compassionate
and faithful. Thus the natural compassion we feel for
one another has its roots in the compassionate Christ
living within us. Not only that, none of us is perfect.
We are all poor and needy, no one is sufficient to themselves.

> Yes, I saw clearly that our Lord rejoices with pity and
> compassion over the tribulation of his servants. And on
> each person that he loves and wants to bring to bliss he
> lays something that, in his eyes, is not a defect, yet
> makes them to be humiliated, scorned, mocked and
> rejected in this world . . . And then I saw that every
> natural compassion that anyone has for a fellow
> Christian is due to Christ living within; and every bit of
> the self-emptying that he revealed in his Passion was
> shown again in this compassion.

RDL 28.3, 4

The suffering Jesus has compassion on our weakness
and failures. In fact they are integral to life, no one escapes

them. Christ Crucified bears the world's sin, accepts all its pain and sorrow. We must learn to do likewise.

To return to God in contrition is a step only once removed from offering others the compassionate love, acceptance and forgiveness we have received ourselves. Henri Nouwen writes, commenting on Rembrandt's painting of the *Return of the Prodigal Son*:

> When I first saw Rembrandt's *Prodigal Son*, I could never have dreamt that becoming the repentant son was only a step on the way to becoming the welcoming father. I now see that the hands that forgive, console, heal, and offer a festive meal must become my own.[1]

Real converts always write the story of their conversion as a discovery of mercy, so that they learn to create mercy for others in their turn. The welcoming hands symbolize the welcoming heart.

As contrition enables a person to move from self pre-occupation to self-acceptance, so compassion enlarges the heart, wounds it, breaks it open for others.

St Thérèse of Lisieux, like Julian another apostle of the mercy of God, was aware of her own weakness in such a way that it made her an excellent novice mistress. She understood her novices 'from the inside', from the point of weakness, and so refused to judge. Instead she sought to nurture.

> I realized that for the most part all souls have the same battles, yet no two souls are exactly alike . . . Each soul therefore must be dealt with in a different way . . . our own tastes, our own preferences must be forgotten, and we must guide souls not by our own particular way but along that path indicated by Jesus.

. . . What would happen if an ill-instructed gardener did not properly graft his trees; if, without understanding the nature of each, he should try, for instance, to grow roses on a peach tree? The tree, which had been vigorous and, perhaps, gave promise of much fruit, would simply wither away.

How important it is to be able to recognize God's claims on the individual soul, even from early childhood, so that instead of anticipating or hindering it we might, rather, second the action of grace in the lives of others.[2]

The humility that enables us to respect difference is the only way to help others grow and change according to their own particular temperament and personality. The secret is to communicate love, respect and acceptance, and this can only be done by an authentic and humble heart beating in the breast of the person who accompanies. It means having a heart modelled on the open heart of Jesus, within which Julian sees a large space, wide enough to accomodate all in peace and rest (*RDL* 24).

There is a story told of a group of American soldiers in the Second World War. One of their number was killed in an enemy ambush and his mates wanted to give him a decent burial. Remembering a small church they had seen nearby, they approached the old priest and asked if he would conduct a burial service for their comrade. The priest agreed to lead some prayers. However, as the dead man was not known to be of any particular faith he refused to bury him within the white fence that marked the cemetery area of consecrated ground. Instead the priest offered burial just outside it. Saddened, the soldiers complied. Next day when they returned to say a final goodbye to their friend they could not find the grave. On being questioned the old priest replied: 'I went to bed and couldn't sleep. I kept wondering what God would really wish. In the end I got up. I couldn't move the grave so I moved the fence. Your friend is now inside with everyone else.'

Let's be ready to move the metaphorical fences we put up to keep others out, and give everyone the space and dignity they deserve – not just in death but in life as well.

Compassion as Listening

In her lifetime Julian was not known as a visionary or as a theologian, she was known as a wise counsellor. We know this from *The Book of Margery Kempe*, who writes of encountering Dame Julian as she seeks help and direction on her own spiritual path.

First Margery tells us that she went to see a Carmelite friar-hermit in Norwich called William Southfield. However, his assurances do not fully satisfy her, so she approaches 'Dame Jelyan' the anchoress, and remains with her for several days. Julian here is willing to give the person who comes to her all the time she needs. She does not try to rush the garrulous and self-doubting woman sitting before her. A response can then flow from listening to the whole tale, not just a truncated version fitted into a 'therapeutic hour', remembering of course that Margery lived many miles away in Lynn, and travelling in those days was both expensive and slow.

True, the friar has reassured Margery that she is on the right path, and Margery has felt comforted. But Julian is more discerning, helping Margery to trust her own experience and the inspiration of the Spirit in her. Margery needs to know that she can go forward confidently and fulfil her deepest desires as long as they are not contrary to the worship of God and the good of her fellow Christians. A single heart can trust that all is well. Even the tears that worried Margery and caused her to be despised by most 'head-centred' people Julian sees as a gift from God, nothing to be ashamed of. In other words, the emotions are not to be set aside in the search for God. In fact, we see Julian giving Margery the teaching found in her own book: that upon everyone God loves there is placed a burden that causes them to be judged and seen as imperfect by others, whereas in God's sight there is nothing to blame. This 'wound' is actually a gift, something positive rather than negative, which can be used for good.

Julian seems to want to free Margery of her persistent self-doubt and encourage her in the way of confidence and freedom. It must have been a great relief for Margery to hear Julian's words of wisdom, cast aside as she so often was and deemed a creature of mere emotion.

Julian shows herself as a woman able to listen, which is itself a form of compassion. It enables others to contact their own story and find in it the leadings of God's providence. How many others must have gone to Julian's window and come away comforted as well as challenged. Julian is able to assure Margery that the Spirit of God is at work as long as all leads to love, trust, purity. The devil has no power over the humble person so there is nothing to fear. Wanting to do right is what matters, not always getting it right!

Compassion as Powerlessness

In Julian's time the hermit or solitary was usually a lay person who had no vested interest in the hierarchical Church or any particular religious Order. Julian is very clear that her focus is on her 'even Christians', others like herself who are 'ordinary' and whose path to God is in the lay state, even though their way of living may differ from hers.

The vocation of hermit-counsellor means having an openness regarding the outcome of another's spiritual journey. It is to enable the other to find and walk his or her own personal path. Unlike a novice director in a community it is not to discern whether someone is called to a particular Order, for example, or even called to persevere in a vocation that seems impossible to follow in the actual circumstances in which someone finds themselves.

Caryll Houselander, a lay woman who counselled many who came to her for spiritual help, was acutely aware that her insights might not be in full accord with the 'official' line that an ordained minister might feel compelled to give. In the first two letters quoted below she is counselling a woman who wants to separate from her husband. In the other she sympathizes with someone in a second marriage, contracted outside the Church, who cannot bring herself to leave the person she loves, even though she is denied reception of the Sacraments on account of this. To the first woman Caryll writes:

> I do feel desperately sorry for you . . . unhappily there are only a few priests who are able to feel compassion for us poor devils when we have to do the right thing which is usually so utterly hateful to our tormented and

twisted human nature. Also, in some cases – all, probably; yours certainly – right is not always so simple. If, after praying and trying in earnest to make a good job of your marriage, you still find the only result is that you are getting to hate your husband, or to feel as if you do, owing to the constant aggravation of his presence, I should have thought that some compromise in the way of a separation would be the way to cause the least sin and misery to all in the end. I may be immoral to say this, but I can't think that a situation which you have struggled and prayed to make tolerable, in vain, and which really does lead to loathing, can be endured indefinitely . . .

I will write you again, a more considered letter. But don't let me lead you astray. Remember, my dear, I give advice that is rather more human and sympathetic than orthodox, and I not only temper the wind to the shorn lamb but also to the neurotic sheep, whose need seems greater. But the root reason is that I dare not give unctuous and rigid counsel to anyone, because I am so profoundly and always conscious of being a sinner myself, not in imagination but in reality and with a ghastly accumulation of irrefutable proof. Consequently I dare not say to people, 'You must do this because it is right,' knowing full well that if I were in their shoes I would do something very much more wrong than they would.[3]

There is more of this correspondence, but towards the end, after the break has been made and the woman concerned wonders whether she is now free to be 'useful', Caryll cautions her as follows:

I would not worry over leading a useful life; there is nothing better or as good as bringing up your child . . . People who are, or think they are useful, with a capital U, are a real menace, they usually wreck the lives of every sensitive person for miles. One ought not to be useful, only just human and spiritually beautiful. God can fix things if we just become pliant and easy-going and don't try to do the job instead of Him.[4]

With the second correspondent Caryll again looks at the particular situation (that of a second marriage) and leaves the woman free to make her own decision, with Caryll's support and acceptance of whatever may transpire.

I must say I am glad, selfishly, that I could not come to see you, because I could not have brought myself to give you what I presume would have been the 'right' advice: I should have been weak, I should have felt too deep a sympathy with you and too much compassion for your husband.

Your problem was an abnormally hard one and only sanctity could really drink the cup offered you: but God knows our hearts and the strength of the things that assail us and the meaning of all that is incomprehensible to us. I am sure that His mercy is surrounding you . . .

I only beg of you one thing – namely, do not cease to trust in God's love and mercy for you . . .

No, you don't seem 'dreadfully weak' to me; I only wonder how you managed ever to be so dreadfully strong – I could not have done what you did for a week!

You are so right to go to Mass and pray, and so brave in the way you face facts and do not try to twist things, in spite of such awful provocation. I am sure you will be given grace in abundance and the whole thing will come right.[5]

It is because both Julian and Caryll have known first the wound of contrition, the union in weakness and sinfulness that is part of our humanity, that they are able to counsel from a position of compassion, not judgement. In the hierarchy of the Church they have no standing. Their power lies in their utter powerlessness to do anything but love, listen and 'let be'.

Compassion as Intercessory Prayer

The medieval hermit was expected to live an intense life of intercession. The hermit life is not for spiritual self-absorption. The *Ancrene Riwle* maps out a practical programme of intercessory prayer by which the anchoress will consider and pray for multifarious intentions. She is to embrace the whole world, praying for the afflicted and oppressed, sinners, the poor, the wretched, orphans and widows, those in peril on the sea, the dying and all who mourn their passing.

Those who counsel others often feel compelled to hold those they accompany before God in prayer. It is a way to draw strength and light from a power beyond the self. Caryll often assures her correspondents that she prays for them, and she encourages them to pray in their turn:

. . . In the meantime, the only thing that I can see that will help you is to learn to love yourself, to forgive yourself, by looking outwards towards God, by accepting the fact that you are loved by Infinite Love, and that if you will only cease to build up notions of the perfection you demand of yourself, and lay your soul open to that love, you will cease to fear . . . I can only pray for you and beg you to turn your face to this immense love and power, and cast all your fear upon it.[6]

To pray for others is to carry them lovingly in our hearts and minds. Contemplatives receive many requests for prayers from the most disparate kinds of people who long to know that someone cares for them in this way. Openness to God turns our hearts naturally outwards. True contemplatives are not willing to remain in selfish peace and let the rest of the world get by as best it can while they remain undisturbed by the world's pain.

Availability, the willingness to listen, to respond sensitively, to be honest and open about feelings and emotions, are all forms of intercessory prayer, in that they put us in touch with others whom we carry before God in our hearts. We give and receive the Spirit of God through our relationships, spiritual and natural. Saints have stressed the importance of friendship and followed it through in action: Francis and Clare of Assisi, Francis de Sales and Jeanne de Chantal, Teresa of Avila and John of the Cross, Thérèse of Lisieux and Sr Mary of the Trinity.

We have to know how to receive love as well as to give it. When we experience this not just in theory but in practice we are more ready ourselves to carry others, even at cost. Love is indivisible. Loving God, loving people, loving all creation are interrelated. Whoever loves, loves all that is, or it is not real love but self-serving manipulation. There is a story told by Father Flanagan, the founder of Boys Town, of a young boy who arrived carrying his even younger brother on his back. To the enquiry as to how he had managed to walk so far with such a load he had merely replied. 'But Father, he ain't heavy. He's my brother.' We carry one another in prayer and in service, and love makes all burdens light.

> For God is all that is good (as I see it) and God made all that is made, and God loves all that is made. Therefore, whoever loves all fellow Christians for God's sake, loves all that is made. For in humankind that shall be saved is comprehended all, that is – all that is made and the Maker of all. For God is in us and God is all. And I hope, by the grace of God, that whoever sees things in this way shall be truly taught and mightily comforted, if in need of comfort.

RDL 9.2

Compassion as Spiritual Motherhood/Fatherhood

Julian, with her emphasis on God, and specifically Jesus, as mother, can enable us to enter more fully into the concept of spiritual motherhood that comes from suffering with others, as Mary suffers with Jesus because of her great love. Suffering and love are two sides of the same coin. A listening ministry is to enter into the pain of another and be there with them as they try to find a way forward. It is a form of birthing that enables the other to come into being in a new way. However, some who carry a degree of 'parental baggage' may be put off by the imagery of spiritual motherhood and see it as possible spiritual 'smotherhood'.

Here Julian is a wise guide, for her image of Jesus as mother is of one who not only cherishes but also chal-

lenges and trains her child according to its age and
development. There is real appreciation of the child as
'other'. Julian writes:

> This fair and lovely word 'Mother' is so sweet and
> gentle in itself, that it cannot truly be said of anyone
> or to anyone except him, and to him who is the true
> mother of life and of all things. The properties of natu-
> ral motherhood are natural love, wisdom and know-
> ledge, and this is God. Though it is true that our
> physical giving birth is but little, humble and simple
> compared to our spiritual birth, yet it is still he who is at
> work when his creatures give birth. A kind, loving
> mother who knows and understands the needs of her
> child, guards it most tenderly, as the nature and state of
> motherhood demand. And always as the child grows in
> stature she changes her methods, but not her love.
> When it gets older she allows it to be chastised in order
> to break down its faults and to enable the child to
> accept values and graces. This, along with everything
> that is good and lovely, is our Lord's work in those who
> do it.

> *RDL* 60.8

Perhaps Julian herself was a mother who had brought
up children, or a woman who had known good mothering
in her own childhood. At the very least she had noticed the
difference between good and bad parenting.

What draws people to the hermit should be a sense that
here is someone who will nurture the other person by
encouraging growth rather than dependence. Modern
hermits are pointed out as men and women who seem to
attract others to themselves as listeners and guides,

because they are independent persons who have made their own journey and found their own particular balance.[7]

Louf writes that many people today are wanting a word from God, a guide to the spiritual life, whether they are specifically 'religious' or not. Faith is not primarily about catechetical instruction but awakening another to the life of God, and that can only happen when the guide is also in touch with God and with life. Real spiritual companions are more than teachers. They are themselves the teaching, their whole lives are the message.[8]

Someone once asked a college professor what the Church needed so that they could decide on their studies according to that need. The reply came back, 'Don't ask what the Church needs. Ask what brings you to life and do that. Because what the Church needs most of all is people who have become fully alive.' Only those who are alive in this way can awaken and foster life in those who approach them for guidance.

A relationship in which the gift of spiritual fatherhood or motherhood is released in the guide, and the gift of discipleship is released in the one who comes for guidance, involves tenderness and toughness. Tenderness and toughness are qualities of a love based on real communication; they cannot be equated with a mindless pat on the back and a few pointers to good living. A true spiritual relationship is always a relationship of speaking the truth in love.

The wound that love opens, the wound of compassion, is decisive in the listening, the loving, the healing, that are part of genuine companionship. It is a love that accepts all things in the other, including weakness and sin. A diet of unattainable ideals is not the nourishing bread of real love, though this may be easier to offer, for it sidesteps involvement in vulnerability.

Julian, in her desire for the wound of compassion, desires a relationship that nurtures love for God and love for others at the deepest level of spiritual motherhood – the level of the true self and the true God who loves us just as we are, and yet also wants us to be all that we can be.

The Second Window

Not surprisingly the wound of compassion is symbolized by the second window in Julian's cell, the window to which others can come for counsel; the window where she offers hospitality to those who seek from her a word that will guide, help and heal. And from the account of her meeting with Margery Kempe we see her as listening, respecting, enabling the other to come to their own decision. Such is the good spiritual guide.

In the best known icon of Julian we see her at her cell window. Her elbow rests on the sill and her left hand is on her cheek, symbolic of attentive listening. Her other hand strokes her cat, for hermits are known to have an ability to relate to the whole created world. Julian's cloak is pink, the colour of wisdom, her robe grey to symbolize her age, for wisdom comes from life experience, gained through the years. Her head is covered with the black veil of a dedicated life.

Julian is an icon of the one who cares, who listens, and who enables others also to grow as compassionate human beings. She listens. She loves. Thus she bears life. And she encourages us to do the same.

Space to Reflect

Be merciful, just as your Father is merciful. Do not judge and you will not be judged; do not condemn and you will not be condemned. Forgive, and you will be forgiven; give, and it will be given to you. A good measure, pressed down, shaken together, running over, will be put into your lap; for the measure you give will be the measure you get back.

Luke 6.36–38

Compassion – the Measure of Love

A compassionate heart is one of God's greatest gifts, but it is usually given in and through the circumstances of ordinary life. The book of Ruth is a wonderful story of compassion being worked out in the lives of two women, a woman of Israel and her Moabite daughter-in-law. Ruth's devotion to her mother-in-law, Naomi, means that she goes with her into a new land. Once there, Naomi's care for Ruth enables the younger woman to affirm herself and fulfil her own destiny in her turn. The sensitive care these two women have for each other enables both to grow and change within the confines of an outwardly simple life. There is no overt intervention of the Divine, but we can see God's ways being worked out through human relationships and human love.

The book of Ruth is very short, only four chapters. At some point over the next few days read it and trace the lines of providence at work as two people relate to each other and their environment in ways that foster mutual respect and compassion.

How does their generosity towards one another both

change and fulfil them? (The old English word 'ruth'
means compassion, though we usually only use it in its
negative form of 'ruthless'.)

Passion and Compassion

Julian sees Mary as the image of the compassionate
person. This is because Mary is willing to suffer with and
for her Son. The mother who stands at the foot of the
Cross is the mother who takes all humanity to her heart,
because she loves all those whom her Son loves. As Julian
suffers when she sees Jesus suffer, so she realizes that
the more we love the greater our capacity to suffer with
and for others. It is a natural gift which we are called to
develop through grace and through practice.

> In [Mary's ability to suffer] I saw the substance of natu-
> ral love, developed by grace, which [God's] creatures
> have for him. This natural love was most supremely and
> surpassingly shown in his sweet mother. For as much as
> she loved him more than all others, her pain surpassed
> all others. For the higher, the stronger, the sweeter love
> is, so is the sorrow greater of one who sees the body of
> a loved one suffer.
>
> RDL 18.1

How can your own natural love for another person be
expanded by grace to include someone to whom you are
not naturally attracted? Name in your heart someone you
love and someone you wish to love more.

St Elizabeth of Hungary

Elizabeth of Hungary (1207–31) grew up at the court of her future husband, Louis of Thuringia. From her early years she showed an exceptional compassion towards all who suffered through poverty, hunger or neglect; and her husband, to whom she was happily married, supported her in her charitable works. But this was not only a natural gift, it was a gift developed by grace over many years. It matured throughout her life and came to full flowering in her widowhood. It was because Elizabeth loved Jesus that each person she encountered revealed a different aspect of him. She did not give of herself only to the grateful and deserving but to all without distinction. Elizabeth lived when Francis of Assisi was preaching the gospel as a poor itinerant, and he became her model. As Francis had kissed lepers, so Elizabeth embraced an identification with the poor, humble Christ whom she served in serving others with 'tender hands', while regarding them with 'tender eyes'.

Scriptural Meditation

Zion was saying, 'The Lord has forsaken me,
my God has forgotten me.'
Can a woman forget her nursing child
or have no compassion on the child of her womb?
Even these may forget, yet I will not forget you.
See, I have inscribed you on the palms of my hands.

Isaiah 49.14–16

Prayer

O Divine Master,
Grant that I may not so much seek
to be consoled as to console,
to be understood as to understand,
to be loved as to love.
For it is in giving that we receive,
it is in pardoning that we are pardoned,
it is in dying that we are born to eternal life.

Attributed to St Francis of Assisi

Notes

1 Nouwen, H., *The Return of the Prodigal Son*, quoted in O'Laughlin, M., *Henri Nouwen: His Life and Vision*, Orbis Books, 2005, p. 142.
2 Quoted in Martin, C., *A Memoir of my Sister St Thérèse*, trans. Carmelite Sisters of New York, Gill & Sons, 1959, pp. 3–4.
3 Houselander, C., *The Letters of Caryll Houselander*, ed. M. Ward, Sheed & Ward, 1973, pp. 66–7.
4 Houselander, *Letters*, p. 69.
5 Houselander, *Letters*, pp. 35–6.
6 Houselander, *Letters*, p. 116.
7 Colegate, I., *A Pelican in the Wilderness*, HarperCollins, 2002, pp. 237–8.
8 Louf, A., *Tuning into Grace*, DLT, 1992, p. 81.

5

Julian's Window on to the Sanctuary and the Wound of Longing

*J*ulian qualifies her request for the third wound with the adjective 'unshakeable'. Any longing will not do. It must be focused. It must be based on the truth. And it must be pursued over the long term.

Biblical Foundations

If any word could encapsulate the theme of many of the psalms it would be longing. The desire for God is all-consuming. To seek the face of God, to discover God in life and in prayer is the one thing necessary.

> O God, you are my God, I seek you,
> my soul thirsts for you;
> my flesh faints for you,
> as in a dry and weary land where there is no water.
> So I have looked upon you in the sanctuary,
> beholding your power and glory.

Because your steadfast love is better than life,
my lips will praise you.
So I will bless you as long as I live;
I will lift up my hands and call on your name.

Psalm 63.1–4

As a deer longs for flowing streams,
so my soul longs for you, O God.
My soul thirsts for God, for the living God.
When shall I come and behold the face of God.

Psalm 42.1–2

In the vagaries of history, in tragedy and exile, Israel's
trust in God has to be maintained. Providence is always at
work. Those who have eyes to see and ears to hear find
God in places where God was thought to be absent. God's
plans for us are always good. 'All shall be well' for those
who persevere.

For surely I know the plans I have for you, says the Lord,
plans for your welfare and not for harm,
to give you a future with hope.
Then when you call upon me and come and pray to me,
I will hear you.
When you search for me, you will find me;
if you seek me with all your heart,
I will let you find me, says the Lord,
and I will restore your fortunes
and gather you from all the nations
and all the places where I have driven you, says the Lord,
and I will bring you back to the place
from which I sent you into exile.

Jeremiah 29.11–14

Only God can reveal Godself to us. Our part is to seek that we may find, ask in order to receive, knock that the door may be opened to us – the door that leads into the mystery of God (cf. Matthew 7.7–8).

Embracing Our Longings

In her youth Julian had desired a vision of the crucified Christ. It was through this longing for a personal relationship with God, based on love and compassion for the Crucified, that Julian would grow in her spiritual life and in her own vocation to solitude, prayer and presence to others.

Julian's love for Christ would lead her from the life of a pious woman living in her own home to the cell of an anchoress. And such a vocation could only be sustained by persevering in the path she had chosen, or rather the path that she believed God had chosen for her.

It is longing and desire, not tranquillity, that characterizes the seeker. And desire needs to be worked at and worked for. It opens us up to another dimension as a 'wound' in need of healing. Contemplation is not perfect physical and mental equilibrium. 'The more God wants to give the more God makes us desire,' writes John of the Cross. God must stretch us so that our capacity to receive the divine grows until we cry out because of the pain and emptiness we experience.

'Our God is a consuming fire,' and my filth crackles as he seizes hold of me; he is 'all light' and my darkness shrivels under his blaze. It is this naked blaze of God that makes prayer so terrible. For most of the time we can persuade ourselves that we are good enough, good as the next person, perhaps even better, who knows? Then we come to prayer – real prayer, unprotected prayer – and there is nothing left in us, no ground on which to stand.[1]

St Francis of Assisi longed for God so intensely that eventually his body bore the wounds of the crucified Christ. His flesh was transformed even as he continued to give himself to lepers, to the poor, to the preaching of the word of God and the service of his brother friars.

St Thérèse of Lisieux echoes John of the Cross in saying that 'It is confidence, and confidence alone, that leads to love.' We must truly trust that God will satisfy all the longings of our heart. Therefore it behoves us to desire well and desire much. Few people could be said to have sought the goal of union with God with the energy and originality Thérèse brought to the task. At the end of her short life she was able to say, 'I have sought nothing but the truth,' and she allowed the truth to take her to places she might rather not have visited had she chosen to be left to her own limited resources.

Teresa of Avila in her turn points out that it is not rest but activity that characterizes the person in the seventh mansion, the mansion of union. Such a one is ever on the watch to do more for God and to enable others to love God more, even at cost to one's own comfort. It is the old story that we cannot give what we do not have. Growing closer to God brings others along with us. Selfish introspection is foreign to the lover of God who is consumed by longing for the divine Lover, and wants to share that love with others through compassion and tenderness.

Writing for Carmelite novices, the poet Jessica Powers

changes an earlier metaphor for holiness – that of a candle slowly burning in the solitude of a cathedral – to: 'a maiden racing towards a sole desire / with garments glowing and her face on fire'.[2]

However, we are creatures of time, sometimes happy, sometimes sad, sometimes well and sometimes sick, sometimes grateful for all we have received, at other times resentful at all we have been denied. Sustaining desire does not come easily to us. It cuts deep. It leaves us bleeding and wounded, and it eventually cauterizes the wound. It opens up our capacity to relate to God, to others and to the immensity of the truths of life that cannot be contained in a small mind and heart.

This longing can also be paralleled with other forms of longing – the search for meaning, for faith, for something to give our lives a value beyond themselves. Great scientists, philosophers, artists, musicians have had to sustain their commitment in the long term. No amount of talent in a musician, for example, can dispense with the hours of practice necessary to perfect the professional performance.

To embrace, own, sustain and nurture our longings is the way to wholeness.

Truly our lover desires our soul to cling to him with all its might and to cling evermore to his goodness. For of all the things the heart could think of, this pleases God most and soonest helps the soul to prayerfulness. Our soul is so preciously loved by him who is highest that it is far beyond the comprehension of creatures. That is to say: no created being can fully know how much, how sweetly, and how tenderly our Creator loves us. And therefore we can, with God's grace and help, remain in spiritual contemplation, endlessly marvelling at the high, surpassing, immeasurable love which our Lord in his goodness has for us. So we may reverently ask from our Lord all that we want; for our natural will is to have God, and the good will of God is to have us.

We can never stop wanting to be his and longing for him until we possess him in the fullness of joy; then we will desire nothing more. He wants us to be completely occupied with knowing and loving him until such time as our longing is completely fulfilled in heaven.

RDL 6.5–6

Julian knew about longing. She understood its costliness during her long years of reclusion. But she had confidence that what she wanted would be given to her if only she held out and did not settle for less. For love is indeed something 'costing not less than everything'.

Desire and the Image of the Holy Face of Jesus

I want to look at Julian's vision of the face of Christ as a way into the mystery of longing and desire. In her Second Revelation Julian gazes at the face of the crucified Jesus and sees there all the pain and humiliation of his suffering. As she watches, dried blood covers first one half of the face, then the other. And she looks with a great longing to discover what this means.

[W]ith my bodily sight I saw in the face of the crucifix that hung before me and at which I continually gazed, part of Christ's passion. I saw there insults, spittle, dirt, bruises, many long-drawn-out pains more than I can tell, and frequent changes of colour in his face. Then I saw how half the face, beginning at the ear, was covered with dried blood which formed a kind of crust as far as the middle of the face. After that the other half was covered in the same way, while the first crust vanished just as it had come.

This I saw bodily, but it was clouded and dim, and I wanted more light so as to see more clearly. Then I was answered in my mind: 'If God wants to show more he will be your light; you need no other.' For I saw him and I sought him.

We are now so blind and foolish that we are unable to seek God until the time when, in his goodness, he shows himself to us. And when, by grace, we do see something of him, we are moved by the same grace to seek him with ever greater longing, so as to see him more joyfully. And so I saw him and I sought him. I had him and I lacked him. And this shall be our ordinary life, as I see it.

RDL 10.1–3

As Julian ponders the changing face of Jesus her thoughts turn to 'Veronica's veil', supposedly kept in Rome as a relic and exhibited to pilgrims on certain feasts. According to legend, a woman named Veronica (*vera icon* – true image) went forward to wipe the face of Jesus on his way to Calvary. As a reward the image of Jesus' face was imprinted on the cloth she had used. From an act of charity a true representation of the suffering Saviour was given to the world.

But Julian has heard (or possibly even seen if she has been on pilgrimage to Rome herself) that the image on the cloth shows Jesus, not handsome and Godlike, but dark with pain and wasted with sorrow. How can that be? Is not Jesus the loveliest of all people to look upon? No, says Julian. The face is as it is because Jesus has borne all our sorrow, allowed himself to be taken as of no account, in order that we might be restored to the divine likeness lost by sin.

The journey to wholeness is for us a journey of transformation. We have to seek, suffer and trust. Seeking is as good as seeing. The process is as necessary as the end result. So we must trust steadfastly in the presence and transforming power of a love that often shows itself to us as dark and unbeautiful.

Faith means trusting in the darkness. The face of God will not always be seen by us as radiant and beautiful. It will instead be mediated through the 'Veronica image' of suffering. But no matter how God is revealed to us we must continue our search.

Many people give up the spiritual journey when the way gets difficult and stony. They do not realize that though the face God shows to us may change, the God whose face it is remains faithful.

St Thérèse of Lisieux developed a special love for the face of Jesus as depicted on the veil of Veronica simply because it was of someone 'without beauty, without majesty' (Isaiah 53.2) and she was trying to come to terms with the mental deterioration of her beloved father. She was determined that in this difficult time she would accept God in whatever way God came to her, even when unrecognizable; as her father himself was unrecognizable as the Papa she loved, a man who no longer knew his daughter or himself and was hidden away in a mental hospital.

Later, after the whole tragic episode was behind her, Thérèse could write that she was glad to have suffered.

But while she was actually suffering all she could do was hold on blindly while weeping in anguish. She was convinced that Jesus was in this painful experience and she would recognize his face in it where others saw only unmitigated disaster.

> O remember that your divine face
> Was always unknown to your own people;
> But you left your sweet image for me
> And, you know it well, I did recognize you . . .
> Yes, I know you, all veiled in tears.
> Face of the Eternal One, I discover your charms.[3]

Longing for God, seeking God, seeking truth, seeking one's true calling, have to be sustained through all kinds of weathers. It is so easy to wait until we feel well, to wait until we feel spiritually uplifted, to wait until we have our lives in order before we continue our quest. But the saints teach us that we must seek continually, no matter what aspect of Christ's face is shown to us. The dark and light are no indication of whether or not we are pleasing to God.

God is here and God is now. Attention to God in prayer is to gaze upon the face of the Beloved in whatever guise it is shown to us.

> Pray wholeheartedly, even though you do not feel like it, for it is a very profitable thing to do even if you don't feel that way . . . even though you feel nothing, yes, even when you think you cannot do it. For in times of dryness and barrenness, in times of sickness and weakness, your prayer is most pleasing to me, even though you may find it rather tasteless.

RDL 41.4

[86]

To long is to pray and to seek. Not just now and then but continually.

Longing and Gratitude

'With prayer goes gratitude. Thanksgiving is a blessed thing in God's sight,' writes Julian (*RDL* 41.5). Helping ourselves and others to find matter for gratitude enables us to persevere on the spiritual journey. Thanksgiving can be centred on what God has done in salvation history or in what God has done in our own lives. Gratitude makes us strong, more ready to act rather than taking the stance of helpless victim.

When I was a child my brother and I would visit our grandparents in the summer holidays. They had had a hard life by any standards. They had both left school at 14 without any qualifications, had spent their working lives struggling to make a living and bring up their only child, a daughter who became our mother. She had died in childbirth, leaving them grieving and bereft. Yet Granny would sit at the old upright piano, playing away and singing the song 'Count your blessings one by one . . .' – and these were not empty words. She did count her blessings, for she knew many who were worse off than she was.

'Our Lord doesn't ask for great achievements, only for self-surrender and for gratitude,' writes Thérèse of Lisieux.[4] To be thankful is a quality that can be learned.

What did Julian have to be thankful for? She lived in an era when the plague carried off thousands, when the country was at war, when heretics were burned at the stake, when the Peasants' Revolt ended not in justice for the oppressed but in a bloodbath. Yet there was also the love of family and friends, the possibility of service to others, prayer, a simple lifestyle in her cell, the beauty of nature. We can always find matter for gratitude if we want to, even in the most circumscribed life.

A friend of Caryll Houselander's who lived in the country would often send flowers to brighten her London room. Caryll went into ecstasies over their beauty – cowslips, bluebells, snowdrops, chestnut buds . . . If we can nurture a love of nature we are already in touch with the God who creates and sustains.

> Thank you so very, very much . . . for the simply lovely cowslips, which arrived in such a glorious condition of living yellow light. I also noticed for the first time what a peculiarly lovely delicate green their stems are – what an astonishing variety of greens God does use . . .[5]

As the persecution of the Jews curtailed normal life in Holland during the Second World War, Etty Hillesum could find delight in what made life beautiful even as she was deprived of more and more of what others might find necessary for human flourishing.

> This morning I cycled along the Station Quay enjoying the broad sweep of the sky at the edge of the city and breathing in the fresh, unrationed air. And everywhere signs barring Jews from the paths and the open country. But above the one narrow path still left to us stretches the sky, intact. They can't do anything to us, they really can't . . . We may be sad and depressed about what is being done to us; that is only human and understandable. However, the greatest injury is one we inflict on ourselves. I find life beautiful and I feel free. The sky within me is as wide as the one stretching above my head.[6]

And Etty's last note, thrown from the train as she was taken to Auschwitz with her family in one of the transportations from Westerbork, says that they left the camp singing.[7] We can choose whether or not to develop an 'attitude of gratitude'. In choosing to do just this Etty held on to her human dignity, her search for God and for truth. Circumstances may depress us, but they cannot overcome the one who refuses inner consent.

Longing and Learning

Julian, Thérèse, Caryll, Etty are women who never stopped learning and growing. In all that they write we see the progress of their spiritual journey going hand in hand with their human development, their search for truth, and a willingness to be surprised and challenged by life. To be ready to learn is a sign of longing, and learning generally includes an element of study and hard work. We do not learn just by cruising along haphazardly. The mind and heart must be applied to experience, to Scripture, to culture, to all areas of human existence.

Julian, in writing her *Revelations*, shows how her thinking has developed and matured over the years that elapsed after the writing of her short text to the longer version written 20 years later. This text shows all the signs of having been worked over with effort and deep thought. She links disparate parts of the text to one another. She has most likely learned to write so as to be able to communicate her insights after her near-death experience, and to learn reading and writing when one is older takes much concentration and effort. She 'had the experience' but was determined not to 'miss the meaning' of it all. Thérèse of

Lisieux carefully studied the translations of Scripture available to her and expressed a wish to learn Hebrew and Greek so as to read the Testaments in their original language; such was her unremitting search for truth.

In Judaism study is considered an element of worship. It gives the intellectual stimulus to a life of longing. It is not enough to contemplate the journey, one must set out on the path. Doing and hearing, studying and practising, are interlinked. All spiritual teachers emphasize that prayer and learning go hand in hand, although in the end only prayer can put us in touch with Ultimate Reality.

The more we pray the more learning comes to life. Prayer enables us to be alert to God's presence when life seems dark (*RDL* 43.4). Prayer is also a work that makes us partners with God. Prayer and trust go together (*RDL* 42.2). Julian takes for granted that we are longing to know more about God and God's ways, even though we cannot have all the answers. The one who 'knows it all' beforehand and the one who never embarks on the quest cannot discover new spaces which are meant to be filled with fruits we cannot know in advance. 'It is, as it were, in our moments of openness, in our undefended spaces, that God can find and speak to us'[8] and thus allow our lives to blossom out in unexpected ways.

Making space is one of the works of prayer. The more we pray the more we long for those spaces to be created and filled with 'we know not what'. The more we learn the more we realize we do not know. Yet the further we walk along the path of spiritual growth the more we grow in experiential trust. God is with us enabling us to discover who we really are, and who God is, in the ground of our being.

In today's world many of the old certainties are being

challenged. The language of God and the liturgy does not speak to the present generation. We have to listen respectfully and realize that often a sharing of our own personal journey speaks more powerfully than traditional theology. All the more important then that we are on our own way, not with all the answers but still asking the questions – still learning.

Longing and Living under a Rule

Judaism decrees that the day be interspersed by intervals for prayer. The Jew's garments, food, manner of life, were and are all brought into the orbit of religious faith. Jesus lived as a devout Jew of his time, and his own life would be formed in every aspect by his beliefs which were embodied in a certain way of life.

Monasticism from the beginning has also emphasized that prayer and the search for God need to be supported by a structure that enables a person to keep their focus when feelings of devotion are no longer strong, or even seem to have disappeared altogether. Singing the Divine Office, following the daily timetable of manual work, holy reading, study and private prayer, wearing the religious habit at stated times, all remind the monk or nun of the vows they have undertaken and the obligations the vows impose in practice.

Julian too would have had her own rule of life – either the *Ancrene Riwle* or something similar. She would have a routine that included time for prayer, for earning a living, for being present to those who sought her help, as well as the time she herself set aside for writing. But basically, like so many today, she would be on her own, responsible to

God and to herself as to how she spent her time. No one living a solitary lifestyle can plan a day that does not offer some surprises and disruption of routine. Of course the same thing happens in family and community, but there are others present to share the burden. In solitude one must carry responsibility alone. Julian would need to decide when to prolong her designated time for writing if a reference book needed to be returned to the Augustinian friars nearby. She would have to decide when a person's need was so great when they came for counsel that she should curtail or omit the time she had set aside for personal prayer. She would have to wait upon her maid's return from town before sitting down to a meal.

After more than 35 years in community, it has taken me around 8 years to develop a rhythm of my own, and even that has to be flexible. Human need, one's own weakness, the demands of life, the vocation to listen to others, all modify the daily timetable.

Yet every part of life is sacred. How can we remind ourselves of this? How we eat (I am still a chocoholic, alas!), how we dress, how we pray, what kind of books we read, all tell us something about ourselves and are all part of the person we are which belongs to God and which should reflect our true self.

I feel that there is a need to help people find and celebrate their own particular vocation, to name it and embody it in a way of living that is balanced yet growthful. In my contact with others called to the solitary life I see an opportunity for transitional moments and moments of choice to be incarnated in symbol and ritual. We may feel imprisoned in our old ways of being or in the place we find ourselves physically or spiritually. Life may be hard, yet with Julian we can also believe that God is leading us on to fullness of joy (*RDL* 77.4). Naming this belief and trying to live by it, finding God's goodness in all things, the humblest physical need as well as the brief gifted moments of contemplative surrender, is worth working for and receiving with gratitude.

The Third Window

The third window of Julian's cell, the window that looks out upon the sanctuary of the church and through which she receives Communion several times a year on great feast days, is obviously the window of our connection with God. It is the narrowest window of all, and yet it opens out on to the widest horizon.

The first window opens upon the world of nature and physical necessity, the second window on to contact with others and their problems. But the third window is the God-window, and God is the whole reason for Julian's life as an anchoress.

Yet Julian, and we ourselves, need all three windows. They are the orifices, the 'wounds' by which we connect with reality. Through them we move from loneliness to hospitality; from fear of ourselves, fear of others, fear of God's disapproval, to acceptance and inner peace.

In solitude Julian finds her true self in all its aspects, and, as Jung says, in finding our true self we find God.

Repentance and sorrow bring us back to the reality of who we are, enabling us to return to the God who loves and accepts us without reserve. Compassion enables us to encounter others with empathy since, knowing our own weaknesses and sins we are never surprised by weakness in others, nor are we eager to pass judgement on them. In longing for God we realize our incompleteness and so remain humble and grounded in truth, ready and willing to grow and to change.

In her most famous vision Julian sees the world in her hand, round and very small, the size of a hazelnut. The hazelnut symbolizes all that is, all the beauty of creation, all the wonder of what it means to be human. It is the world that God has made, that God loves, and that God keeps in being. But in itself it is too small to satisfy the immense longings of the human heart.

What God wants above all else is that we just come to God simply, humbly and in a homely way, saying:

God of your goodness, give me yourself,
you are enough for me.
I cannot ask anything less to be worthy of you.
If I were to ask less I should always be in want.
Only in you have I all.

RDL 5.4

Space to Reflect

Ask, and it will be given to you; search, and you will find; knock, and the door will be opened for you. For everyone who asks receives, and everyone who searches finds, and for everyone who knocks, the door will be opened.

Matthew 7.7–8

Focusing our Longing

Nearly all the saints seem to have found a way to keep their longing for God alive through dark times. And they

did this through developing a special love for one aspect of
the life of God, Jesus or the Spirit. For Teresa of Avila it
was the person of Jesus as he confronted the woman of
Samaria, and she boldly asked him to give her the living
water he had promised. Teresa tells us that she had a
picture showing the woman at the well, with the words
'Domine, da mihi aquam' beneath it. And she would continually repeat the woman's request, 'Lord, give me some
of that water.' For Thérèse of Lisieux it was the image of
the Holy Face that became her icon. For Elizabeth of the
Trinity it was the mystery of the Trinity. For others it has
been Jesus Crucified, Jesus the child of Bethlehem, God as
creator and sustainer, God as living Spirit.

Take some time to discover and name where your
spiritual attraction finds concrete expression.

Choose a Gospel story to which to return constantly,
and which will help you focus your attention when prayer
is difficult. Each time you return to it you will then find
deeper layers of meaning.

Choosing Jesus

Julian seems to have found her particular focus not just
in Jesus Crucified and all that the mystery of the cross
came to mean to her, but in the very person of Jesus. In her
Shewings she is tempted to look heavenwards to the
Father and divert her attention from the crucified Christ.
But she chooses not to go down this path. Instead she
chooses Jesus to be her heaven.

In this way I was taught to choose Jesus for my heaven,
whom I saw only in pain at that time. I wanted no other
heaven than Jesus, who will be my bliss when I get

there. It has always been a great comfort to me that, by his grace, I chose Jesus to be my heaven throughout all this time of his Passion and sorrow. This taught me that I should always do so, choosing only Jesus to be my heaven through thick and thin.

RDL 19.3

Write a prayer to name and claim your own 'heaven' on earth – that particular aspect of God or Jesus that appeals most to you.

Blessed Charles de Foucauld

Charles de Foucauld (1858–1916) was orphaned at a young age and brought up by a grandfather who indulged his every whim. In adolescence Charles lost his faith, joined the army and continued to live scandalously, wasting his inheritance in giving wild parties and keeping a mistress. It was his encounter with religious Jews and Muslims when he went as an explorer to Morocco that brought him once more into contact with people of faith, and he was impressed. At the age of 27 Charles underwent a deep conversion experience that would give direction to the rest of his life. His attraction was to Jesus at Nazareth, a poor worker among other workers. No formal religious life seemed to meet Charles' needs, though he tried the Trappists, tried living as a handyman in Jerusalem, and eventually found his place as a hermit in the Sahara. There he died, murdered by the tribesmen he had loved and served for the last 15 years of his life. Only after his death did others follow his example as 'Little Brothers and Sisters of Jesus', poor workers among other workers. In his spiritual notes Charles wrote:

Reminder to let Jesus' heart live in me,
so that it is no longer I who live,
but Jesus' heart living in me
as he lived at Nazareth.

Through his love for Jesus at Nazareth Charles sustained his longing to the end.

Spiritual Meditation

Bless the Lord, O my soul,
and all that is within me, bless his holy name.
Bless the Lord, O my soul,
and do not forget all his benefits –
who forgives all your iniquity,
who heals all your diseases,
who redeems your life from the Pit,
who crowns you with steadfast love and mercy,
who satisfies you with good as long as you live
so that your youth is renewed like the eagle's.

Psalm 103.1–5

Prayer

Father, I abandon myself into your hands,
do with me what you will.
Whatever you may do, I thank you;
I am ready for all, I accept all.
Let only your will be done in me
and in all your creatures.
I wish no more than this, O Lord.
Into your hands I commend my soul;
I offer it to you with all the love of my heart,

for I love you, Lord,
and so need to give myself,
to surrender myself into your hands without reserve
and with boundless confidence,
for you are my Father.

Charles de Foucauld

Notes

1 Beckett, W., 'Simple Prayer', *Clergy Review*, February 1958.
2 From the poem 'Young Maidens Running' by Jessica Powers, in Powers, J., *Selected Poetry*, ed. R. Siegfried and R. Morneau, Sheed & Ward, 1989, p. 58.
3 From the poem 'Jesus my Beloved, Remember', in Thérèse of Lisieux, *Collected Poetry*, trans. D. Kinney, ICS Publications, 1995, p. 129.
4 Thérèse of Lisieux, *Autobiography of a Saint*, trans. R. Knox, Fontana, 1958, p. 180.
5 Houselander, C., *The Letters of Caryll Houselander*, ed. M. Ward, Sheed & Ward, 1973, p. 162.
6 Hillesum, E., *An Interrupted Life and Letters from Westerbork*, trans. A. J. Pomerans, Henry Holt & Co., 1983, pp. 144–5.
7 Hillesum, *Interrupted Life*, p. 360.
8 Wittenberg, J., *The Three Pillars of Judaism*, SCM Press, 1996, p. 42.

Epilogue
A Personal Odyssey

*A*s the years have gone by in my own life I have come to look upon Julian as a friend and an inspiration on my own path.

From childhood I had wanted a life lived for God that encompassed every aspect of my being. That is why both Judaism and the monastic life appealed to me. I knew that alone I could do nothing. With others all things were possible, but it would have to be a way of life that included all of life, and not just a Sunday observance.

At 18 I entered a Franciscan Congregation that was strongly monastic in orientation. It was a real culture shock and I hated every moment of my postulancy (the first six months when one is not a sister but a person living alongside and experiencing the life for oneself). What kept me going was simply pride – I had told my father I wanted to be a nun against his wishes, and I wasn't ready to give up easily. Another element was fear. Superiors were all-powerful, one dared not displease them.

But everything changed once I received the habit. Now I was a nun! Now everything could be given to God! Now I knew what to do as there were rules for everything, from the smallest thing to the greatest, from how to pin on the novice's veil to how to behave in chapel. I had a new name, new clothes, a new start. It felt good to be me. Sometimes I felt overwhelmed with joy at being among sisters who shared a common life and common ideals. I remember walking across the garden from house to chapel before five every morning, the wind blowing my long choir veil, the day barely beginning, and repeating the words 'I thank you God, for the beauty of the morning and the joy of my heart.'

But such a life can actually mask deep anxieties and insecurities. Trying to live up to great ideals when one is very young pushes a large part of the self underground. Keeping perpetually busy with work did not help me to confront reality. As long as I did what I was supposed to do and behaved as a nun was supposed to behave I was all right. But when that failed I knew subconsciously that I had nothing to fall back on, no real spiritual foundation for discovering either God or my true self. Underneath the well-trained exterior I felt confused and angry, even as I continued to be truly grateful for my religious vocation.

I loved the sisters – they were my 'family'. In many ways I loved the life. But in the years that followed Vatican II there was a lot of unrest among us as a group. It was as if we were sitting on a pressure cooker, waiting for it to explode at any moment. It was stressful trying to combine so much work with a life of monastic observance and the full Divine Office. Open discussion of problems was discouraged. Something would have to 'give'. (It did in due course, but by that time I had moved on.) I knew changes needed to be made in the Congregation and I felt they were not changes I could live with. I had always felt drawn to Carmel and a life of prayer, so after a lot of heart searching I asked to transfer to the Carmelite Order. In an enclosed community I would not have to do what I felt unable to do. Or so I thought.

Enclosed life was not another culture shock such as my first entrance had been. I felt at home from the beginning. There was love and trust, kindness and a balanced regime. It was where I truly wanted to be. But I was not prepared for solitude and its demands. What did I have to sustain me inside when alone? Nothing. And so I tried to surrender to what my vocation demanded. Again I felt I belonged yet did not quite belong. I was integrated into a close community life where my gifts were given scope to develop. I studied, prayed, learned to value solitude and tap into my own inner resources, initiated others into the life as novice mistress myself. The years in enclosure were some of the happiest and most fulfilling years of my life. Yet as time went by I began to feel 'caged'. I wanted to be close to people, to welcome the marginalized, the unloved, in simple ways that enclosure made impossible.

As I worked on myself and my journey with the help of a trained therapist I was gradually able to articulate my real hopes and desires. But how could I follow them? I was living a vowed life and intended to be faithful to it. Then the possibility of a new direction was mooted and I knew I must either follow my dream or choose a known security and safety. I chose the dream.

Moving to Aylesford was suggested, and I accepted, not knowing what that would mean in practice, yet feeling deep inside me that it was the right thing to do. Aylesford is an important place of pilgrimage in Kent, belonging to Carmelite friars, a place where all can come and where there might be a need for someone just to 'be there', listening, praying, befriending.

I made a great 'leap in the dark' setting out in trust, not knowing in advance how things would work out for me. It was the Father Provincial who, after three months, suggested that I be consecrated as a Carmelite solitary attached to the Shrine. Thus I could stay and lead a life beside the friars with my own rhythm of prayer, solitude and presence to others.

Even as it was suggested I suddenly 'knew' that this was the solution. I had not thought of being a hermit, but now God was offering me this vocation. Unlike my other forays into religious life which I had chosen myself, this was God offering me something new – *God's* choice for me. I recognized that it 'fitted'. And it has indeed proved to be exactly right.

I am not a priest, nor even part of the Carmelite community. I live beside the friars but apart from them, with my own life of simple presence and listening. I also do some retreat work and spiritual direction, having the freedom to accept invitations for these if I can fit them into my schedule. Of course this demands personal responsibility, flexibility, a balancing of the various components of my lifestyle.

I continue to say the full Office, some of it with the friars, the remainder on my own. I eat with the guests and pilgrims so that they know me as a friend and universal sister. Then I have the hours of prayer and reading in my cell or one of the chapels, my solitary walks, my time to relax. Like Julian I belong to a particular place and am available to those who come.

What is more, since embarking on this path I have discovered that there are many hermits and solitaries in today's Church, each of us different, yet each finding our own way forward. One sister I know subsists on her pension and has the Blessed Sacrament in her house so that she can take Communion to the sick. Another paints icons and lives in a caravan. Another lives a more strictly eremitical life in an adapted garden shed. Wales seems to be heaving with hermits everywhere, some following an Orthodox way of life, others inspired by Charles de Foucauld, Franciscan, Carmelite or Dominican spirituality. Another solitary lives in a small cottage in a pilgrimage village and earns her living by hospice nursing. Sometimes we have the possibility of contact and sharing, but this is optional.

In this way of life I see Julian as an inspiration to all of us. She is not tied to one particular spirituality, she is for everyone. Her wounds of contrition, compassion and longing form part of our journey and our heritage as solitaries. But even for those not called to the official eremitical life she can teach us much of what it means to seek God and in so doing come to know our true self and celebrate our own being as loveable, cherished and free.

For the hermit's cell is an image of the person, with access to practical living, relationships with others, and connection with the Divine. From how we use these creatively and sensitively will emerge our unique vocation. And the wounds of failure, of rage, of grief, of anguish, of sin, will form part of the pattern of who we are, and ultimately become badges of honour. For we are known by our wounds rather than by the unmarked and smooth areas of the self. 'All shall be well.'

Space to Reflect

'I am the true vine and my Father is the vine-grower. He removes every branch in me that bears no fruit. Every branch that bears fruit he prunes to make it bear more fruit. You have already been cleansed by the word that I have spoken to you. Abide in me as I abide in you.'

John 15.1–4

Abiding in God

Each one of us is invited to abide in God and to bear fruit, each in our own way and within our own life. Often it is only looking back that we can see how God has led us. While we are in the thick of things there can seem nothing but chaos and confusion. For each of us the story of our life is still in process, for:

No star is ever lost we once have seen
We always may be what we might have been.

The saints who have written their own autobiographies stress that they are 'singing the mercies of the Lord'. God brings good from everything if we are open; but we can only see the hand of providence when we reflect in retrospect.

Note the main transitions and choices in your own life that have brought you to this point in time. What choices do you need to make so that you continue to follow your star?

Our Life – Gift and Task

If life is a gift it is also a task. We must decide what we will do with this gift, how we will use our talents, how relate to others, how reach out or withdraw. What Julian sees is that our life can never be completely fulfilled here on earth. We alternate between falling and rising, longing and listlessness. Only God remains steadfast in love and acceptance of who we are and who we are called to be.

> [God revealed himself] as if he were on pilgrimage: that is to say that he is here with us, leading us and staying with us until he has brought us all to the bliss of heaven. He revealed himself several times, as I have said, chiefly as residing in the human soul. He has made the human soul his resting place and his royal city. And from this glorious throne he will never get up or move away permanently. The place where our Lord dwells is wonderful and magnificent, and therefore he wants us to respond quickly to the touch of his grace, rejoicing more in his unbroken love than sorrowing over our frequent falls. For out of all the things we can do in our time of penance, the one that gives him most honour is to live gladly and joyfully for love of him.

> *RDL* 81.1–4

Make a list of things you want to thank God for in your life. Make another list of the things you regret. Then remember Julian's assurance that God wants us to rejoice rather than sorrow over failings, for God's love is a love that cannot be broken by sin.

Ruth Burrows

Ruth Burrows (1925–) is a contemporary spiritual writer and guide who has been a Carmelite nun for many years. She is also a woman who has had to wrestle with a problematic and sensitive temperament, community pressures, bereavement, disappointment, in fact all that makes up a specific human life. Around the age of 50, feeling that she had really nothing much to celebrate, she was persuaded by a friend to write her life story, which she did in an account published under the title *Before the Living God*. This writing enabled her to marshall her thoughts and express her experience in such a way that all her life so far was affirmed. Far from being a failure, her very handicaps had turned into gifts; the feeling that she was 'not religious enough' was offset by her growth in humanity. Towards the end of her book she writes:

> To cut ourselves off from maturing processes, to shirk growth under cover of the cliché 'God alone' is, in fact, to escape from God. God is not glorified in half-persons. The more we open ourselves to life, to let the waves of life flow over us, allowing ourselves to feel, to suffer, to wonder, the more we are opening ourselves to God.[1]

Life is life is life – mine, yours, ours, and in and through our life we discover the God who loves each one uniquely and takes joy in our being.

Scriptural Meditation

Listen to me. O house of Jacob,
all the remnant of the house of Israel,
who have been borne by me from your birth,
carried from the womb;
even to your old age I am he,
even when you turn grey I will carry you.
I have made, and I will bear;
I will carry and will save.

Isaiah 46.3–4

Prayer

My God, I thank you
for the glory of my life.
                    Ruth Burrows

Notes

1 Burrows, R., *Before the Living God*, Sheed & Ward, 1975, p. 118.

Appendix
Further Information for Those Interested in the Solitary Life

There are a number of associations and publications that exist to support hermits and solitaries, whether single or married, lay or religious. This list is not exhaustive.

Fellowship Charitos Inc. (ecumenical)

For lay or religious solitaries, sharing support and a monthly newsletter *The Flag*.

email: fellowshipcharitos@yahoo.com

www.fellowshipcharitos.com

Contact: Fellowship Charitos, Inc.
           650 South 3rd East no. 404
           Salt Lake City
           UT 84111
           USA

Raven's Bread: Food for those in Solitude
(online newsletter)

www.op.org/ravensbread/

Contact: Raven's Bread
           18065 Hwy 209
           Hot Springs, NC 28743
           USA

Fellowship of Solitaries (ecumenical)

A fellowship for lay and consecrated hermits and solitaries.

www.solitaries.org.uk

Contact: Mr John Mullins,
           4/5 Akeld Cottages
           Wooler
           Northumberland NE71 6TA
           UK

Catholic Hermits (RC)

For all those who practise or are interested in solitary consecrated life within the Roman Catholic Church; and for those who value solitude, whether chosen or imposed through circumstances.

email: Catholic_Hermits@yahoogroups.com

The Society of Franciscan Pilgrims (RC)

A vowed lifestyle that can be lived in various ways by the single or married, young or mature; living at home but part of a supportive community in the tradition of St

Francis. There is a special emphasis on reconciliation between Christians.

For further information, tel. 01653 552240

www.soc-franciscanpilgrims.co.uk

Association of Hermits and Solitaries of Julian of Norwich

A small association for women and men who seek or follow a more formal consecration to the solitary life, giving information and personal support.

Contact: Sr Elizabeth Obbard
          The Friars
          Aylesford
          Kent ME20 7BX
          UK

Tel. 01622 714122

Bibliography

All biblical quotations are from The New Revised Standard Version of the Bible, copyright 1989, Division of Christian Education of the National Council of the Churches of Christ in the United States of America.

The quotations from the *Revelations of Divine Love* (RDL) by Julian of Norwich are taken from the unpublished translation of the Paris Manuscript by Josef Pischler MHM, edited by E. R. Obbard.

Poetry extracts from *The Selected Poetry of Jessica Powers* published by ICS Publications, Washington DC (formerly published by Sheed & Ward). All copyrights © Carmelite Monastery, Pewaukee, WI. Used with permission.

Books

Aelred of Rivaulx, *Rule of Life for a Recluse*, in *Treatises and Pastoral Prayer*, Cistercian Fathers Series, no. 2, Cistercian Publications, Kalamazoo, 1971

Allchin, A. M. ed., *Solitude and Communion: Papers on the Hermit Life*, SLG Press, 1977

Alison, J., *Raising Abel*, Crossroads, 1991

Bradley, R., *Julian's Way: A Practical Commentary on Julian of Norwich*, HarperCollins, 1992

Burrows, R., *Before the Living God*, Sheed & Ward, 1975

Clay Rotha, Mary, *The Hermits and Anchorites of England*, Methuen and Co., 1914

Colegate, I., *A Pelican in the Wilderness*, HarperCollins, 2002

Dalrymple, W., *From the Holy Mountain*, HarperCollins, 1998

Eldred, J., *Changed Lives: Miracles of the Passion*, Harvest House, 2004

Elizabeth of the Trinity, *Complete Works Volume Two*, trans. Anne Englund Nash, ICS Publications, 1995

Guenther, M., *Holy Listening: The Art of Spiritual Direction*, DLT, 1992

Heuk, Doherty C. de, *Poustinia*, Ave Maria Press, 1975

Hillesum, Etty, *An Interrupted Life and Letters from Westerbork*, trans. A. J. Pomerans, Henry Holt & Co., 1983

Houselander, C., *The Letters of Caryll Houselander*, ed. M. Ward, Sheed & Ward, 1973

Jantzen, G., *Julian of Norwich: Mystic and Theologian*, SPCK, new edn, 2000

John of the Cross, St, *Collected Works*, trans. K. Kavanaugh and O. Rodriguez, ICS Press, 1991

Jones, A., *Soul Making: The Desert Way of Spirituality*, SCM Press, 1986

Kemp, J., *The Spiritual Path of Caryll Houselander*, Paulist Press, 2001

Kempe, *The Book of Margery*, trans. B. A. Windeatt, Penguin, 1985

Leyser, H., *Medieval Women: A Social History of Women in England*, Phoenix Press, 1995

Little Brothers and Sisters of Jesus, *Cry the Gospel with Your Life*, Dimension Books Inc, no date

Louf, A., *Tuning into Grace*, DLT, 1992

Markides, K., *The Mountain of Silence: A Search for Orthodox Spirituality*, Doubleday, 2001

Martin, C. (Sr Genevieve), *A Memoir of my Sister St Thérèse*, trans. Carmelite Sisters of New York, Gill & Sons, 1959

Merton, T., *Solitude and Love of the World*, Burns & Oates, 1997

Moltmann-Wendel, E., *Rediscovering Friendship*, trans. J. Bowden, SCM Press, 2000

Nomura, Y., *Desert Wisdom: Sayings from the Desert Fathers*, with an introduction by Henri Nouwen, Orbis Books, 1982

Nouwen, H., *Reaching Out*, Collins, 1976

Obbard, E. (ed.), *Medieval Women Mystics: Selected Writings*, New City Press, 1999

O'Laughlin, M., *Henri Nouwen: His Life and Visions*, Orbis Books, 2005

Powers, J., *Selected Poetry*, ed., R. Siegfried and R. Morneau, Sheed & Ward, 1989

Rogers, C., *A Way of Being*, Houghton Mifflin, 1980

Rogers, C., *On Becoming a Person*, Constable, 1967

Sheldrake, P., *Spirituality and History*, SPCK, 1991

Sulivan, Jean, *Eternity, My Beloved*, trans. Sr F. E. O'Riordan, River Boat Books, 1999

Teasedale, W., *A Monk in the World*, New World Library, 2002

Thérèse of Lisieux, *Autobiography of a Saint*, trans. R. Knox, Fontana, 1958

Thérèse of Lisieux, *Collected Poetry*, trans., D. Kinney, ICS Publications, 1995

Thorne, B., *The Mystical Power of Person-Centred Therapy*, Whurr, 2002

Underhill, E., *Mystics of the Church*, James Clarke & Co. Ltd, 1975

Waddell, H., *The Desert Fathers*, Fontana, 1962

Wilson, M. R., *Our Father Abraham: Jewish Roots of the Christian Faith*, Eerdmans, 1989

Wittenberg, J., *The Three Pillars of Judaism*, SCM Press, 1996

Wyler, S. M., *Settings of Silver: An Introduction to Judaism*, Paulist Press, 1989

Articles

Beckett, W., 'Simple Prayer', *Clergy Review*, February 1958

Fusco, R., 'The Contemplation of Christ Crucified in Julian of Norwich', *Studies in Spirituality*, 2003

Jantzen, G., 'Julian of Norwich: Desire and the Divine', Lecture given at Norwich Cathedral, 1996

Law, S., 'A Room of her Own: Julian, Prayer and Creativity', Annual Julian Lecture, 2003, The Julian Centre, 2003

Louf, A., 'Humility and Obedience in Monastic Initiation', *Cistercian Studies*, 1983

McAvoy, J., 'To Be Satisfied: Julian of Norwich and the Meaning of Atonement', *Studies in Spirituality*, 2003

McClean, J., 'Teresa of Avila and Self-Knowledge: Psychology and the Spiritual Journey', *Mt Carmel Review*, Jan–March 2005

Obbard, E. R., 'Julian, a Woman in Transition', Annual Julian Lecture, 2000, The Julian Centre, 2000

Stockton, E., 'Lay Hermits', *Compass Theology Review*, vol. 34, no. 2, 2000, pp. 46–50.

Thorne, B., 'Mother Julian, Radical Psychotherapist', Annual Julian Lecture, 1993, The Julian Centre, 1993